CAMBRIDGE MUSIC HANDBOOKS

Nielsen: Symphony No. 5

CAMBRIDGE MUSIC HANDBOOKS

GENERAL EDITOR   Julian Rushton

Cambridge Music Handbooks provide accessible introductions to major musical works.

Published titles

Nielsen: Symphony No. 5

David Fanning

Senior Lecturer in Music, University of Manchester

CAMBRIDGE
UNIVERSITY PRESS

PUBLISHED BY THE PRESS SYNDICATE OF THE UNIVERSITY OF CAMBRIDGE
The Pitt Building, Trumpington Street, Cambridge CB2 1RP

CAMBRIDGE UNIVERSITY PRESS
The Edinburgh Building, Cambridge CB2 2RU, United Kingdom
40 West 20th Street, New York, NY 10011-4211, USA
10 Stamford Road, Oakleigh, Melbourne 3166, Australia

First published 1997

Printed in Great Britain at the University Press, Cambridge

Typeset in 10½/13pt Monophoto Ehrhardt

A catalogue record for this book is available from the British Library

Library of Congress cataloguing in publication data

Fanning, David (David J)
Nielsen, Symphony no. 5 / David Fanning.
p.   cm.   (Cambridge music handbooks)
Discography: p.
Includes bibliographical references (p.   ) and index.
ISBN 0 521 44088 2 (hardback) – ISBN 0 521 44632 5 (paperback)
1. Nielsen, Carl, 1865–1931.   Symphonies, no. 5, op. 50.
I. Title.   II. Series.
ML410.N625F36   1997
784.2′184–dc20   96–46053   CIP   MN

ISBN 0 521 44088 2 hardback
ISBN 0 521 44632 5 paperback

Contents

For Jo

Acknowledgements

Sentimental though it may sound, this book is intended in part as a gesture of thanks to the composer of music which has played a huge part in my life. Quite simply, it has helped me to keep sane. Others may disagree. But I should like to thank a number of individuals who share my love of Nielsen and who have offered me their time, expertise and hospitality. These include the Nielsen scholars Robert Simpson, Mina Miller, Torben Schousboe, Jørgen I. Jensen, Niels Martin Jensen, and Michael Fjeldsøe; the Chairman of the Carl Nielsen Society of Great Britain, Jack Lawson; his counterpart in Denmark, Henning Tjørnehøj; the staff of the Royal Library Copenhagen, especially Birgit Bjørnum, Klaus Møllerhøj and Susanne Thorbek; and the conductors Jonathan del Mar, Ole Schmidt and Sir Simon Rattle. My thanks also to Martin Parker for processing the musical examples and to Penny Souster and Caroline Murray of Cambridge University Press and Professor Julian Rushton for steering the book through to publication. I remember with particular gratitude those students whose reaction to Nielsen may be summed up as 'where have you been all my life?', and I am grateful to my colleagues at Manchester University for their personal and professional support. I acknowledge the assistance of the university's Staff Travel Grants in the Humanities and Social Sciences, which enabled me to visit Copenhagen in the summers of 1991 and 1995, as well as an award from the *Carl Nielsen og Anne Marie Carl-Nielsens Mindelegat*. My wife, Jo, knows the depth of feeling which lies behind my dedication of this book to her.

Abbreviations

CNB	Møller, I. E., and Meyer, T., *Carl Nielsens breve* [Carl Nielsen's Letters] (Copenhagen, Gyldendal, 1954)
CNS	Simpson, R., *Carl Nielsen: Symphonist*, 2nd edn (London, Kahn and Averill, 1979)
DB	Schousboe, T., ed., *Carl Nielsen: Dagbøger og brevveksling med Anne Marie Carl-Nielsen* [Carl Nielsen: Diaries and Correspondence with Anne Marie Carl-Nielsen], 2 vols. (Copenhagen, Gyldendal, 1983)
FS	Catalogue numbers for Nielsen's music established by Dan Fog and Torben Schousboe in *Carl Nielsen: Kompositioner* (Copenhagen, Nyt Nordisk Forlag–Arnold Busck, 1965)
KM	Meyer, T., and Petersen, F. S., *Carl Nielsen: Kunstneren og mennesket* [Carl Nielsen: The Artist and the Man], 2 vols. (Copenhagen, Nyt Nordisk Forlag, 1947–8)
LM	Nielsen, C., *Living Music* (London, J. and W. Chester, 1953)
MB	Telmányi, A. M., *Mit barndomshjem* [My Childhood Home] (Copenhagen, Thaning & Appel, 1965)
NC	Miller, M., ed., *The Nielsen Companion* (London, Faber, 1995)

Introduction

The 'victory-through-struggle' symphony is an enduring monument of Western culture, albeit one which is now looking somewhat dilapidated and which has become encrusted in ways its creators could not have foreseen. Fifth symphonies seem to have been particularly vulnerable. Beethoven's C minor set the process in motion. Idolised by Nielsen as by practically every composer with ambitions to compose symphonies, it was the first great darkness-to-light journey in music, the first to allow separate movements to interpenetrate, the first to unify them motivically with a view to reinforcing dramatic cohesion; or if not literally the first, it was the first so to embed itself in the consciousness of audiences and composers. But it also received the most famous 'encrustations', first when Beethoven's pupils Czerny and Schindler disagreed over whether the famous four-note opening motif stood for the song of the yellow-hammer or Fate knocking on the door, and later when the Allies in the Second World War used the same motif to signify Victory.

None of the other great victory-through-struggle or dark-to-light Fifth Symphonies has acquired the iconic force of Beethoven's, but each has been felt, or forced, to stand for something ideologically concrete. Before the 1939–45 War Hitler had already appropriated the finale of Bruckner's Fifth.[1] Before that Sibelius's Fifth, along with his symphonic output in general, had been taken as the embodiment of Viking virility – a view the composer was content to endorse but which eventually provoked a violent critical reaction.[2] Nearer the present day, in 1971 Luchino Visconti's film *Death in Venice* reinterpreted the 'Adagietto' of Mahler's Fifth, turning the composer's love-song for his wife into an emblem of decay and morbid homosexual frustration. And over the years Shostakovich's Fifth has ceased to be understood in terms of the composer's supposed subtitle 'A Soviet Artist's Practical Creative Reply

1

to Just Criticism' and has come to stand for something close to the opposite, one myth thus being substituted for another.[3]

Nielsen's Fifth has been more fortunate. It has become sufficiently well known to have made its mark, but not so over-played as to seem hackneyed, so over-commentated as to have become the target of myth-making, or so over-praised as to have provoked a backlash. It has not been besmirched by the entertainment industry, commandeered by political propagandists, or hijacked by intellectual cliques. Unmistakably dealing with life-and-death issues, in a manner at once stylistically engaging and structurally sophisticated, it is the kind of work which may actually catch admirers on the rebound from over-exposure to other great twentieth-century symphonists with comparable ethical concerns.

In an age which has witnessed human 'struggle' on a previously unimaginable scale, the concept of 'victory' in art-forms has come to seem barely defensible, a cheapening of the issues. Some would argue that that was already the case in 1921 when Nielsen was composing his Fifth Symphony. But composers are not prisoners of history, they are shapers of it. At least they can be, if they share Nielsen's determination to tackle human issues head-on and to find a musical language and structure with which to do them justice. In such cases engagement with an archetype whose heyday is apparently over can give a composer's work a special edge. Such is the case with Nielsen's Fifth.

It is widely held to be the summit of his achievements. Deryck Cooke, celebrated for his Performing Version of Mahler's Tenth Symphony, is even said to have dubbed it 'the greatest twentieth-century symphony'.[4] Be that as it may, the point probably does not need hammering home. The time has surely passed when a crusade needed to be fought on Nielsen's behalf. In 1952 when the first edition of Robert Simpson's masterly study appeared,[5] it was a different matter, and this may account for Simpson's somewhat dismissive remarks about other composers and trends. He toned down these comments by the time of the revised edition in 1979, but if nothing else they had served to stir up discussion of a composer few had previously thought to put in the front rank. Meanwhile a huge boost to Nielsen's reputation came in 1962 when Bernstein's recording of the Fifth Symphony appeared – it remains arguably the most inspiring version on record (see chapter 4 below). Less conspicuous, but indicative of the steady growth of interest in and admiration for Nielsen, was

Stephen Walsh's contribution to the article 'Symphony' in the 1980 *New Grove Dictionary of Music and Musicians*, which ranged him alongside Mahler and Sibelius as more or less equally important symphonists around the turn of the century.[6] Seventeen years on, that assessment seems not unrealistic, with a dozen complete or near-complete cycles of Nielsen's symphonies currently available on Compact Disc and a steady stream of concert performances. The scholarly community is also beginning to catch up with the musical world at large, with a Complete Edition of the music well under way, an international symposium recently published, and a new popular biography about to appear.[7]

If a crusade is no longer needed, an aggressive moral stance on Nielsen's behalf also runs the risk of being counter-productive. Journalistic appreciations of Nielsen continue to clutch at descriptions such as 'healthy', 'invigorating', 'life-giving' – not (presumably) out of copycat thoughtlessness, but because those terms come spontaneously to mind when the music is played.[8] They are all adjectives the composer himself used and approved of, and they reflect what has been dubbed, with reference to the philosopher Henri Bergson, his 'vitalist' outlook.[9] Before jumping to the conclusion that this could be one of the few manifestations of twentieth-century idealism still worth upholding, it may be worth remembering that in Nielsen's time such terminology was often used in the context of a reactionary moralising that few of us today would wish to endorse.[10] It has even been suggested that: 'The consequential continuation of the *Espansiva* [Nielsen's Third Symphony] would have led to the art which our century's later totalitarian regimes extolled.'[11]

There is a balance to be struck here. Certainly there is a danger of Nielsen enthusiasts under-playing the many-sidedness of his musical personality, and that is the point of raising the whole ethical question here. But nor should misappropriation of ideas by later generations in other cultures mean that Nielsen is retrospectively tainted. There is no need to abandon worthy principles just because others have put them into wicked practice. In other words, there is no need to apologise for the ethical content of Nielsen's music, with its anti-decadent slant, provided it is looked at with an open mind. In any case his next symphonies were far more than 'consequential continuations' of the 'Espansiva', as they were affected by unforeseen extra-musical factors, most obviously the

First World War, in which Nielsen saw patriotism transformed into a 'spiritual syphilis'.[12]

Nielsen's high ethical stance remained meaningful in proportion to his awareness of the darker forces which threatened it, and to his artistic strategies for dealing with both poles, which he outlined in his Fourth Symphony ('The Inextinguishable') and perfected in his untitled Fifth. Not that immersion in the inimical forces of Life was anything unusual for a composer on the cusp of late romanticism and modernism. What was unusual was Nielsen's determination to transcend that experience through a process of dynamic psychological growth, mirrored in complex, self-generating musical structures. This is the issue I have tried to keep as the main focus of my book. To do it justice demands, I believe, a 'close reading' of the music, with no apologies for any ideological dimension anyone chooses to read into the enterprise.[13]

Nielsen's Fifth is (or at least should be) an overwhelming experience – for the innocent, the curious and the jaded alike. His capacity to overwhelm is not a matter of emotional suffocation or aural bombardment (though in his first movement there is a conspicuous instance of the latter). Rather it arises from a realisation of humane values, in music which is at once boldly original and deeply rooted in tradition. It is a combination, in other words, of reach and grasp. Nielsen reaches towards the big issues, touching on the most destructive elements that life can throw at us; he proposes that they can be faced, resisted and absorbed, if never truly overcome, by forces within us, provided we can gain access to them. As for grasp, this is evident in the subtlety with which his musical images of good and evil are wedded to long-term structural processes and transformed thereby, elevating generalised anthropomorphism from manifesto to music. To investigate this is, ideally, to make the overwhelming experience more fully and more permanently our own, to ensure that it nourishes the soul rather than passing through like some temporarily invigorating pill. That is the ideal I have tried to keep in mind.

As a preface to the main analytical part of the book I have sketched a historical context for the symphony as a threatened species (chapter 1). But it is my belief that getting to grips with one of the masterpieces of music, as I have attempted to do in chapters 2 and 3, teaches us that the survival of a genre, or, as in this case, of an archetype within that genre, is a matter of individual creative will. Historical pressures may be a challenge, never a veto.

So far as analytical commentary is concerned, Nielsen scholarship has been laggardly.[14] I feel that my own approach remains broadly compatible with Robert Simpson's, and I am proud to acknowledge his influence on its tone and content. His analysis is, however, more than forty years old, and it remained virtually unchanged in the 1979 revision of his book. Its emphasis on tonal schemes and their putative metaphorical force has been as widely criticised as it has been admiringly echoed.[15] It undoubtedly embodies the creative preoccupations of its author, who has since won deserved international acclaim as a composer. Not that one-sidedness or a personal angle are necessarily a bad thing, unless they are mistaken for the only true path to understanding. No doubt my own approach is no less coloured with personal emphases. What I do hope to offer is an equally distinctive view to Simpson's and a more rounded and detailed one than has been available hitherto. Apart from straightforward commentary on the musical surface, this entails a thorough reexamination of Nielsen's handling of harmony and tonality, and an entirely new scansion of his musical paragraphs. For the interest of specialist or specially intrepid readers, reductive analytical summaries are presented in Appendix C. I have also taken into account the Danish musicological perspective, which is mainly interpretative rather than analytical.[16] Very little of this has filtered through into English-language publications (which goes also, surprisingly, for Nielsen's own remarks on the work, translated in Appendices A and B).

From December 1899 on (shortly before the Second Symphony), Nielsen made very few sketches and generally composed straight into a pencil-draft orchestral score.[17] His draft of the Fifth Symphony and his ink fair copy are retained in the Carl Nielsen Collection at Copenhagen's Royal Library,[18] and pertinent information in these sources is incorporated into the two main analytical chapters. Apart from this, the history of the Fifth Symphony's composition, early performances, reception, editions and recordings, is dealt with in chapter 4.

There are two published scores – the first dating from 1926, and a posthumous revision in 1950. Michael Fjeldsøe's scrupulously researched Critical Edition volume, scheduled to appear not long after this book, should become the standard score, and current plans are for his critical commentary to be available on CD ROM. Without attempting to duplicate his findings, I have included a summary of the most conspicuous discrepancies between the 1926 and 1950 scores. This should be of interest to conductors and to owners of the latter publication, which has been the only widely obtainable source for nearly half a century.

No recordings were made of Nielsen's own conducted performances of any of his music, but several conductors can legitimately claim contact with that tradition, and their recorded interpretations throw up many points of interest. These and many other issues of performance practice in the symphony are summarised in chapter 4, in the course of a discussion of all twenty-six recorded interpretations to date.

1

Tradition and renewal

The death of the symphony?

In 1888, the year Nielsen embarked on his first attempt at a symphony,[1] George Bernard Shaw announced that the symphony as a musical form was 'stone dead'.[2] In 1940, fifteen years after Nielsen's sixth and last symphony, the Danish composer Knudåge Riisager published an article entitled 'The Symphony is Dead: Long Live Music!'[3]

It would be easy to scoff: to rub Shaw's nose in the symphonic master-pieces of Nielsen, Sibelius, Elgar and Mahler; to confront Riisager with Shostakovich, Prokofiev and Vaughan Williams; to cite Maxwell Davies, Henze, Górecki, Holmboe, Kancheli, Lutosławski, Sallinen, Schnittke, Silvestrov, Simpson and Tippett as evidence that rumours of the sym-phony's death have been exaggerated.

Even today, however, there are those who would consider that the rumours were not exaggerated at all, or at least that some of the sym-phonists just named have failed to shoulder the full responsibilities of the genre. Perhaps there is indeed such a thing as symphonism by default; perhaps the 'Breath of Symphonists', which Schoenberg claimed to perceive in Shostakovich and Sibelius,[4] is actually an illusion in the twentieth century, the reality being a necrophiliac artificial respi-ration.

The symphony's premature obituarists have had their reasons, and it may be worth playing devil's advocate a little longer. For it can scarcely be denied that individual composers, even whole generations, have expe-rienced symphonic 'crises'. Beethoven himself turned away from the genre in the last fifteen years of his life, and the one symphony he pro-duced in that period (The Ninth, 1822–4) bequeathed huge problems, as well as inspiration, to the next generations of symphonists. When

Eduard Hanslick hailed Brahms's First as its only true successor some fifty years later, he was looking back on a twenty-five-year fallow period during which the symphony was over-shadowed by the symphonic poem and had nothing better to show for itself than Gade, Raff and Rubinstein and the pre-mature essays of Dvořák and Tchaikovsky.

Another fifty years on, in the post-First-World-War context of Nielsen's Fifth, the symphony as it had been understood until that time once again seemed ill-adapted to the prevailing winds.[5] It was not only the traumas of war and the Communist Revolution which defined the *Zeitgeist*. This was also the time of the confirmation of Einstein's theory of relativity (1919), of Freud's *Beyond the Pleasure Principle* (1920), and the publication of Joyce's *Ulysses*, T. S. Eliot's *The Waste Land* and part two of Oswald Spengler's *The Decline of the West* (all 1922). These were all indications that the period from 1815 to 1914, 'the most peaceful and productive years in the history of mankind' as Paul Johnson has provocatively described it,[6] had come to an end, and with it the kind of art forms which had mirrored that century's self-confidence. Beliefs in progress and humanity, which had sustained projects like the symphony, had been dealt a huge blow, and with the reaction came a mistrust of the genre's presumed baggage of elitism, high ethical content, idealism and large orchestral forces – virtually its entire psychological and sociological infrastructure. The Second Viennese School triumvirate now only approached the symphony with its own radically re-defining agendas, as too did Stravinsky. Brevity and chamber scoring were among their innovations, and shrinking of dimensions was taken to an extreme by Darius Milhaud. Late-romantic over-ripeness had given way to a pruning-almost-to-death. Among Milhaud's fellow-members of *Les Six* only Honegger turned to the symphony at all, and that not until the 1930s.

High ethical aspirations in the symphony did survive the death of Mahler in 1911, but not very securely. Schoenberg himself found it impossible to convert his most ambitious symphonic project into reality.[7] Vincent D'Indy, whose Second Symphony of 1903 had been an explicit representation of the conflict between Good and Evil, now enshrined his feelings about the First World War in his pallid Third Symphony of 1916–18.[8] An exact contemporary of Nielsen's Fifth was Roussel's Second Symphony, for whose première Roussel provided a programme (later withdrawn) relating the three movements to different stages of human life.[9] Comparably high ambitions lay behind two Danish symphonies of 1919 – Louis Glass's Fifth (*Sinfonia svastica*) and Rued Langgaard's Sixth (*Det himmelrivende* [The Heaven-rending]); but despite their champions neither work commands repertoire status. Almost the only other symphonies, certainly the only fine ones, to attempt an encapsulation of the experience of war, were Vaughan Williams's Third, the 'Pastoral', premièred just two days after Nielsen's Fifth on 26 January 1922, and Myaskovsky's Sixth, composed during 1921–4 and arguably more bound up with the experiences of the Bolshevik Revolution and the subsequent civil war in Russia than with the war in Europe.

As for the senior established symphonists in the 1920s, Elgar had already fallen into a disillusioned silence; Nielsen himself shifted from the epic line he had pursued in his first five symphonies, and in his last symphony, the 'Sinfonia semplice' of 1925 he consciously confronted the state of crisis he perceived in musical styles and values of the time; Sibelius brought his drive for unity to a conclusion in his single-movement Seventh Symphony of 1924 and went into a thirty-year retreat, the famous 'silence of Järvenpää'. At that time no significant heirs to the nationalist traditions of Eastern Europe were on the horizon. It was the mid-1930s before the Soviet Union produced, by an extraordinary combination of pressures, symphonies which were more than academically still-born or experimentally iconoclastic. Meanwhile a great individualist interested in writing symphonies, like the émigré Prokofiev, did so only by adopting the foreign language of Parisian *style mécanique* (No. 2) or by adapting material conceived for the opera or the ballet (Nos. 3 and 4). Only the 1930s swing of the pendulum back to idealism and large ambitions, albeit in a now more consciously democratic guise, renewed the seed-bed for symphonism in England, America, the Soviet Union, and to some extent France (but not in Germany, and not to any great effect until much later in Scandinavia).

The survival of a symphonist

Nielsen's Fifth stands as a summit of achievement in terms of his personal creative evolution. Yet it is a summit from which the foothills of an ongoing flourishing tradition had been eroded. He not only had to build his symphonic edifice; he had first to mark out his own plot and lay the foundations. This does not mean that the Fifth Symphony was an attempt to reinstate an outmoded past, however. Rather it was an attempt to deal with the present in a manner emulating, at the most fundamental level, the finest that composers of the past had produced in dealing with their present. It was that very capacity to 'deal with' which the post-war *Zeitgeist* in Europe was questioning, and this is the sense in which Nielsen was working against the grain.

What enabled him to do that so effectively was a mixture of character disposition, musical affinities and life experiences. Nielsen inherited his father's gift for mimicry,[10] and he gradually developed it from a personal characteristic into an artistic principle of empathy, which operates on an ever-widening scale in his first five symphonies. He also inherited from both parents a respect for the elemental power of straightforward melody and rhythm. His early musical affinities were with the rhythmic force, will-power and ethical tone of Beethoven, exemplified in the latter's Fifth Symphony,[11] with the melody, harmony and instrumentation of Brahms and Dvořák, and with the Scandinavian accents of Grieg and Svendsen. However radical his later stylistic journeys, he constantly returned to these roots for sources of well-being and energy. They were sorely needed, because the life experiences which helped to shape his musical development created a thrice-deracinated psyche à la Mahler – as a peasant-boy from the island of Fyn among cosmopolitan Copenhageners, as a Dane within European society, and as a late-nineteenth-century believer in the innate goodness of mankind confronted with the traumas of the new century. Each of these uprootings was a challenge Nielsen had to rise to in his life; and his music shows a comparable determination to tap inner sources and rise above external threat.

Nielsen was not entirely alone in his aesthetic or stylistic preoccupations, as the symphonies of Vaughan Williams and Honegger attest.[12] Indeed it was Honegger who, after the Paris concert including the Fifth Symphony in October 1926, told Nielsen, 'You formulated the aims for which we are all striving now, a generation before the rest of us!'[13] Such statements would have made bizarre reading in German-speaking lands and probably still do today. While America and Britain, and to a degree France, have enthusiastically embraced Nielsen, the Germans never seem to have acquired the taste. Admittedly Nielsen never suffered from the Adorno-led backlash against Sibelius's popularity in the 1930s and

40s, motivated in large part by the Finn's adoption by the entertainment industry.[14] But even today there is strong resistance to Nielsen in German-speaking critical and academic circles, as indeed there is to Sibelius and to Shostakovich (who is admitted to the canon by the back door of his supposed political dissidence – a double misunderstanding of his achievement). Perhaps all this ultimately reflects is difficulty in acknowledging that subtlety and richness in music can operate in the horizontal plane, across extended time-spans, as well as vertically, in the harmonic and surface-rhythmic dimensions.

Nielsen as modernist

Be that as it may, there are signs that the Germanic view of music history should be able to accommodate Nielsen in the front rank. His first four symphonies span a quarter-century from 1891 to 1916. This almost precisely coincides with what Carl Dahlhaus, one of the most penetrating historians of nineteenth- and twentieth-century music, has identified as a well-defined era of self-conscious musical modernism.[15] Dahlhaus himself never mentioned Nielsen in his ruminations on music history. But his framework has been elaborated by James Hepokoski in a fine study of Sibelius's Fifth Symphony. Ranging Nielsen and Sibelius alongside Elgar, Puccini, Mahler, Wolf, Debussy, Strauss, Glazunov, Busoni and 'several others', Hepokoski suggests that they all

> sought to shape the earlier stages of their careers as individualistic seekers after the musically 'new', the bold, controversial, and the idiosyncratic in structure and colour. But simultaneously, as sharp competitors in a limited marketplace, they were also eager to attract and then perpetuate the constituent parts of the delivery system [the institutions of art music].[16]

Hepokoski suggests that most of these composers had two-phase compositional careers. The first was 'the active, or competitive phase, ... characterized by the forging of differently accented, individualized languages from the mid 1880s through, roughly, the first decade of the twentieth century'. In large-scale enterprises such as symphonic composition this involved a questioning attitude to inherited gestures and linguistic devices, and a set of 'deformation procedures' departing from, but dependent for their comprehensibility on, the internalised norm of sonata form.[17] The categories of these procedures are (i) the breakthrough deformation (e.g. Mahler I/1 and 4), (ii) the introduction–coda frame (e.g. Elgar I/1), (iii) episodes within the developmental space (e.g. Strauss *Don Juan*), (iv) various strophic/sonata hybrids (e.g. Mahler II/5), (v) multi-movement forms in a single movement (e.g. Schoenberg Opp. 4, 5, 7, 9).[18] Nielsen's Fifth draws on every one of these categories.

The second phase of these 'modernist' careers, in reaction to 'the more radical musical challenges of the years 1907–14', retains the deformation procedures but within the context 'either of disillusioned withdrawal from the "progressive" marketplace or of the last-ditch – but doomed – defence of a beleaguered fortress'.[19] The new factor, according to Hepokoski, is a feeling of having been outflanked by the New Music developments crystallised around Schoenberg and Stravinsky. From now on the orientation of the 'modernists' had to be not only within the German mainstream tradition, with possible nationalist modifications, and not only against the perceived flabbiness of late-romantic decadent sensuousness; it also could not avoid an awareness of the revolutionary developments in Vienna and Paris. For Nielsen this awareness becomes a major factor in the Sixth Symphony, the 'Sinfonia Semplice' of 1925. But in the Fifth it is arguably already a factor in enabling him to confront himself self-critically and define his own territory.

Until recently few commentators outside Denmark have thought Nielsen worth considering in this way as a major figure in the broader sweep of musical history. So perhaps it was natural for Nielsen enthusiasts to react violently by declaring that he stood above all trends and –isms, as a model for a direction that history might have, even should have taken, and maybe still could take. Defensive arrogance notwithstanding, there is something to be said for that view, for Nielsen was undoubtedly sufficiently self-confident to resist any trend he found pernicious or uncongenial. Nevertheless the broad historical résumé outlined by Dahlhaus and Hepokoski is an important contribution to the more rounded context for Nielsen's achievement which has been gradually emerging in recent years. For here was a composer as deeply engaged as any of his contemporaries with the social and artistic issues of his time.

Symphonic polarities

Soon after finishing the Fifth Symphony, Nielsen entertained his pupil Ludvig Dolleris at his elder daughter's house. Dolleris reports that the composer's guard dropped, perhaps through fatigue, and that he explained the work in terms of fundamental dichotomies:

> I am out walking in the country – I'm not thinking of anything in particular... The various motifs are really chaotic, almost accidental – only one of them, the 'evil' motif is used a lot. Then *suddenly* I become aware of myself as a musician: my thoughts take a definite form, impressions flood forth in me – and now everything is singing pleasantly... A solo clarinet ends this large idyll-movement, an expression of *vegetative* (idle, thoughtless) Nature. The second movement is its counterpole: if the first movement was passivity, here it is action (or activity) which is conveyed. So it's something very primitive I wanted to express: the division of dark and light, the battle between evil and good. A title like 'Dream and Deeds' [Drøm og Daad] could maybe sum up the inner picture I had in front of my eyes when composing.[20]

Each of the polarities mentioned here has a history for Nielsen. The contrast between activity and passivity, which was taken up by early commentaries on the work,[21] recalls his very first symphonic plans. Even before his First Symphony (1891–2) he had been investigating the idea of a semi-programmatic symphony with the motto 'You have come from the Earth, you shall return to the Earth':

> Dark and primeval at the beginning, when everything still lies in millennial hibernation. Then little by little movement and life, but still semi-unconscious, and then rising and rising to the highest joy of life. Then back again to the 'dark soil' which wraps us all in its soft, tight cloak; when you fall asleep for ever – eternal oblivion.[22]

In a sense this unrealised project could be said to have come to fruition in the first movement of the Fifth Symphony.

The 'division of dark and light' was a source of constant fascination for Nielsen. In August 1892 he wrote to his wife that he had been impressed by its presence at the beginning of St John's Gospel;[23] and his *Helios* Overture (FS32, 1903) is one obvious example of a piece built on the same contrast.

The 'battle between evil and good' is not difficult to account for either, given that Europe was still reeling from the shock of the war. Denmark, like all the Scandinavian countries, had been a neutral observer, and Nielsen never expressed a partisan view. He did, however, share in the widely felt sense of apocalyptic horror:

> It's as though the whole world is in dissolution... The feeling of nation-hood which hitherto was considered something high and beautiful, has become like a spiritual syphilis which devours the brains and grins out through the empty eyesockets in senseless hate. What kind of bacillus is it that conquers the warring nations' best heads?... It's so unlimited and meaningless that life doesn't seem worth it. But it has to be resisted, like so much evil in the world. One thing I would wish: that this war should not end until the whole civilised world lies in ruins! Now we must do it thor-oughly! Now we must finally finish it off. This must never happen again, therefore it must now be done with a vengeance.[24]

Apart from this remarkable statement, Nielsen was unforthcoming with his feelings about the war and its influence on his music, except to say that, while he was not conscious of it when working on the Fifth Symphony, 'not one of us is the same as we were before' (see Appendix A).

In fact there were two further experiences dating from 1914, which created a subtler, unacknowledged, but more powerful and deeper-rooted polarity in Nielsen's emotional life at the time. These were his estrangement from his wife since the revelation of his infidelities,[25] and his resignation from the conductorship of the Royal Theatre, which pro-pelled him into a freelance existence for the first time in his life. From then until the healing of the marital rift in 1922 his letters show a man torn between his need for peaceful security and a real-life situation which seemed to offer anything but that.

According to Nielsen's famous motto at the head of the Fourth Sym-phony: 'Music is Life, and like it Inextinguishable'. The first part of this motto is invertible: 'Life is Music':

> Everything that reality brought him in to his life... was something he was ready and able to experience as music, and which with his outstanding ability and unceasing instinct he sought to form and present as musical works. Not just hearing and compositional technique were involved here, but everything he himself understood by 'life'.[26]

The context for Finn Mathiassen's statement is an examination of the paradox of programme and non-programme in Nielsen's music and writings. Nielsen's most recent biographer, Jørgen I. Jensen, has gone further, examining national, personal and cultural elements in Nielsen's musical psychology, and even drawing analogies between Nielsen's 'vitalist'-influenced musical programmes for 'The Inextinguishable' and the Fifth Symphony and scientific developments such as those initiated at the time (unbeknown to the composer) by the Dane Niels Bohr, who won the Nobel Prize for Physics in 1922.[27]

Jensen's hermeneutic reading of the Fifth Symphony is the most original and persuasive since Simpson's, and it is worth summarising it at this point. He sees the main motifs of the first movement as embodying national consciousness, love-longing, the feminine, and threat (for further details see chapter 2 below, pp. 21, 36). Their co-existence in the crisis of the side-drum-dominated second half of the movement stands for 'rest in movement, security in change' – a state of mind in which Nielsen's acceptance of crisis conditions gives him a paradoxical sense of hope. Symbols of body (the side-drum rhythm), soul and spirit are here united and separated at one and the same time by the power of music: 'What externally sounds like a drum going amok in the middle of a beautiful elevated melody and puts the whole orchestra against it, is in reality a personal possibility of experience and guarantees that the work really is perceived strictly personally.' If the first movement is the complete realisation of Nielsen's inner life and existential drama, the second then looks out to the world. It is 'composed by a rootless man who despite his many friends was rather alone and yet still wanted to say yes'.[28]

For many years English-speaking commentators on Nielsen have implicitly followed the opposite view, that 'it is a great mistake to suppose that it is an artist's duty necessarily to reflect his time'.[29] The warning holds good to the extent that it is the specifically musical properties of a symphony which elevate it from the level of newsreel commentary to the uniqueness and permanence of a work of art; and my own preference is certainly to apply detailed commentary at this level, rather than to elaborate a biographical or symbolic narrative. But is there any reason not to have the best of both worlds? Biography and national and international history provide the background for the Fifth Symphony, as Jensen and others have argued. Intertextual reference then helps in supplying the musical imagery (largely derived from the representations of the exotic in Nielsen's theatre scores and tone poems, as I shall suggest in the following chapters). That imagery is nurtured by psychological pressures, suggesting broad lines of structural extension. Above all it is inspiration and symphonic know-how – the short-term, mid-term and long-term working-out of musical ideas – which bring a symphonic masterpiece into being. And when a masterpiece is the object in question it both demands and repays the closest scrutiny.

To follow the next two chapters either a score or an extremely detailed memory of it will be needed. Rehearsal numbers refer to the widely available 1950 publication (see chapter 4 below, pp. 83–4).

For the sake of clarity and conciseness I have divided the work into sections. In the first movement, sections **A1** to **A8** make up the *tempo giusto*, **B1** to **B4** the *adagio*. Where extensions and transitional passages are intercalated, these are labelled **A1a**, **A1b**, and so on. The second movement falls into four large sections – the *allegro* (section **A**), the *presto* fugue (**B**), the *andante* fugue (**C**), and the recapitulation of the *allegro* (**D**). From time to time the Italian terms alone will be used to designate their respective sections.

2

The first movement: dark, resting forces[1]

Section A1 (opening – fig. 2, bb. 1–24). Vegetative.

Tempo giusto. Just so. A strict tempo with no commitment as to character. No equivalent this time to *orgoglioso*, *colerico*, or *espansivo* (Nielsen's designations for the first movements of Symphonies 1–3), nor even to an apparently plain *allegro* whose non-committal appearance is belied by the heading 'The Inextinguishable' and a bold motto on the facing page of the score (Symphony No. 4). Nielsen's pencil draft score for the first movement of the Fifth Symphony was headed *All[egr]o moderato*, but whereas in the First and Third Symphonies he upgraded the plain *allegro* of his draft scores to a character marking, here he downgrades it to total neutrality.

This is no character piece then, or if it is, the character is being deliberately withheld. There may be all manner of biographical and intertextual features behind the music, but these are not defining or confining elements. Even the title that appears on the draft score of the first half of the movement – 'Vegetativ' – is one Nielsen chose to suppress when it came to publication.[2] Where the music is coming from is subordinate to what it is and where it is going to. And where it is going to is, even more than usually with Nielsen, an open question. As he was fond of saying, 'Vi aner ikke hvor vi ender' [We never know where we'll end up].[3]

The *tempo giusto* marking is doubly non-committal. Not only is the character unspecified, the sense of pace is too (the metronome mark says nothing about this). But *tempo giusto* suits Nielsen's purpose. The 'strict'-ness defines the arena for a large-scale drama of supra-personal forces; and for the time being the uncharted medium through which we are travelling is as important a phenomenon as the yet-to-be-defined consciousness of the traveller.

Nielsen is sparing but scrupulous with his markings in this movement, and they all carry structural force. In the entire *tempo giusto* phase the only expression marks are *molto cantabile* (fig. 14), where the strings first strive to stem a negative tide and divert the music to a new tonal plane, *poco a poco tranquillo* leading to *tranquillo* at the achievement of this second plane (fig. ^{3}16–16), and *espressivo* for the bassoons' reprise of the first theme (fig. 16^{3ff}). *Espr.[essivo] con tenerezza* for the oboe at fig. 21^3 appears at a crucial stage in preparation for the *adagio*, and a further *tranquillo* and *espressivo* signpost the transition to it at fig. ^{2}24.

If there *had* been a character marking for the opening, what would it have been? *Misterioso*, perhaps, in view of the uncertainty of purpose and direction; or *lontano*, in view of the subdued dynamics and the sense of a veil between ourselves and the music. Perhaps the special nature of the theme defies encapsulation in words, since it lies in the sense of its being neither fully present nor even preparatory, but reactive. If, as Nielsen suggests, the music conveys a state of 'thinking of nothing in particular' (see Appendix B) perhaps that is because there has been all too much to think about in the recent past. Just for the time being we are in remission from those thoughts, from *all* thoughts.

It is one of the great original openings. The originality is not in the static backcloth itself, which is a standard opening gambit passed down from Beethoven's Ninth via Bruckner. It is not in the oscillating string line – Mendelssohn's and Sibelius's Violin Concertos start from a similar gesture. It is not even the fact that this is a minor third oscillation – see the middle section of Musorgsky's 'Baba Yaga' from *Pictures at an Exhibition*. But the fact that the first four bars are a single, minimally inflected line is unique in the previous history of the symphony. We are poised between pure background and potential character, the potential residing entirely in one interval and in one rhythmic value, as yet unorganised into larger units.

It is harmony which determines, or rather withholds, the character of the music. Nielsen embarks on a theme which tentatively probes various harmonic directions – compare the unproblematic opening of *Springtime on Fyn* (see Ex. 1), the cantata Nielsen composed in the middle of his work on the Fifth Symphony and which conveys the benign side of Nature. What is absent in the symphony is as important as what is present. Missing are firm first beats of the bar (compare the sighing

Ex. 1 (a) Fifth Symphony, first movement, bb. 1–8 (b) *Springtime on Fyn*, bb. 1–7

iambic motifs in the first theme of Mahler's Ninth). Missing is metrical definition – or if we hear downbeats in the iambic motif our interpretation is soon contradicted. Missing for a while is any clear tonal definition – possibilities of A minor, C major/minor and D minor are opened up but shied away from, and when F is temporarily confirmed it is arrived at by the back door of the modal flattened seventh, E♭ (b. 11); the first page of Nielsen's draft score shows that he toyed with, but then suppressed, a one-flat key signature. Most conspicuously missing is a bass line which would provide a secure foundation for the harmony. This is a delicate balancing act, this 'thinking of nothing in particular' which must yet hold the listener in thrall.

The iambic rhythm is a crucial component. Even the tempting hairpin dynamics serve, arguably, more as a highlighter for this rhythm than as an invitation to the bassoons to be expressive. The other source whose potential energy will be tapped is the tetrachord descent stepwise from G – see bracketed motif on Example 1. It is used to question the F major cadence and to spark off the harsh C♭ major semiquaver scale in the bassoons (fig. 1^{8-10}), which contradicts F by its tritonal opposite and knocks the violas' oscillation off-balance for the first time.

Here, presumably, is Nielsen's 'starting creature' (see Appendix B). The image is conveyed in music of compelling economy. Indeed every harmony so far touched upon is prophetic of significant tonalities later in the symphony; the only such key not yet touched on (G) will very soon appear. The 'starting creature' is without immediate consequence, however. Its scale comes to rest on the bassoon's basement B flat; the potential plagal cadence to the tonic F evaporates, and the temporarily interrupted stream of consciousness in the violas settles back to normal.

Section A1a (fig. 2–⁴4, bb. 24–40)

The horn call which has been heard in combination with the tetrachord descent will be a vital player in the symphonic drama. So far it has not appeared in a 'pure' state. At its first appearance (bb. 7–8, see Ex. 1) it had a modal mixture ($E_\flat$/$E_\natural$) which provoked an expanded continuation towards the F cadence (bb. 10–11). Then it undermined the F major cadence with a chromatic variant (fig. 1^{6-8}). Now it is finally heard in its pure classical-romantic form and on its archetypal instruments, a pair of horns (fig. 2^{1-3}). The answer is a balancing call on the flutes, and together these pairs dwell on the C/D oscillation suggested at the beginning of the main theme (bb. 5–6) in what is, in the Schoenbergian sense, a liquidation of the first phrase of the bassoon theme.[4]

An oscillation between C and D majors is what the score suggests. But to the ear the effect is not so simple. The flutes are not a literal transposition of the horns; rather, they hover between C and G centres. Overall the impression is not of a clear bitonality but of a unified D mixolydian mode. Viewed another way, the music is resting on an arc of the circle of fifths (embracing D, G, and C) rather than focused at a point on it. At figure 3 this non-committal state of affairs is resolved in favour of G minor, but with dorian inflections, which could also be expressed as a different arc of the circle, shifted one step flatwards to G, C, and F.[5]

The initiating force of the iambic rhythm, together with the starting-point of another descending tetrachord from G and the repetitive circling motion, emphasise that this sub-section is an exploration of the first four bars of the bassoon theme. In effect it is a verticalisation and hence a paralysing of those bars. The interdependence of horizontal and vertical, in aggregates which rest on arcs of the circle of fifths, is as crucial to the idiosyncratic musical language of this symphony as its overall 'progressive' tonal scheme. It is one realisation of a project that Nielsen had envisioned shortly after the Third Symphony, in a letter to Henrik Knudsen of 19 August 1913: 'we should for once see about getting away from keys and yet still having a diatonically convincing effect'.[6]

Ex. 2 (a) Fifth Symphony, first movement, fig. $^{3-2}$4 (b) Third Symphony, third movement, bb. 18–19 c) 'Genrebillede' [Genre picture], FS14, No. 1, bb. 29–30

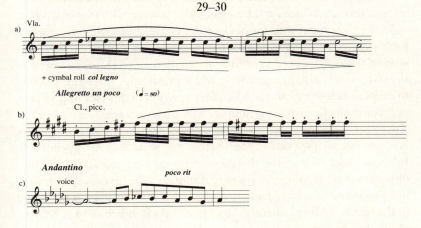

Section A1b (fig. ^{3}4–4, bb. 41–3)

Just as the bassoon's 'starting creature' at fig. ^{3}2 left a potential plagal cadence to F in the air, so the flutes and clarinets now leave us with an unrealised perfect cadence to the same key (fig. 3^5). However, there is one further element of the opening to be explored before any kind of resolution takes place. This is the oscillating viola line, the stream of consciousness which will run almost unbroken through the first 107 bars of the piece until it is replaced by a more malevolent presence, that of the side drum. Its non-committal minor third now reduplicates itself, reaching up to the flat seventh of F and germinating in a lower auxiliary trill, a figure Nielsen had exploited in the third movement of the 'Sinfonia espansiva', and which he had foreshadowed in the love-longing of the first of his Jacobsen songs in 1899 (see Ex. 2).[7] Even without the benefit of hindsight, a sense of premonition or warning is registered, thanks to the extended hairpin dynamic, underscored by a sizzle on the cymbal. The viola line is, in Robert Simpson's words, 'like the wave of a seismograph that reacts to the tremor of earthquakes at vast distances, then settles to its neutral uniformity'.[8] In terms of Nielsen's description, however, this expansion of the line is undoubtedly the 'onde Motiv', the evil motif, in person. The draft score suggests that it may only have arisen in the midst of the compositional process – the motif is pencilled in the margin of the first page, a dozen bars or so before its actual appearance, as though an idea for future use had just occurred to the composer.

In the movement thus far Nielsen has established a kind of template for his symphonic drama, at least for the *tempo giusto*. The template consists of three elements – (a) a thematic statement (**A1**), (b) a shadow of the statement, perhaps in the form of a liquidation, expressing inability to develop or move forward (**A1a**), (c) a reaction to this lack of progress, perhaps in the form of a warning or other token of apprehension (**A1b**). There are eight rotations of these elements up to the *adagio*[9] (where Nielsen 'become[s] aware of [him]self as a musician' – see Appendix B). In some cases two of the three elements may be fused; always their dimensions are flexible; always they respond to the preceding character in a process of ongoing dramatic evolution. It is a concept not unrelated to the 'rotation' form identified by Hepokoski in Sibelius's Fifth Symphony, but on a smaller scale – something in between variation and rotation form, perhaps.[10]

Section A2 (fig. 4–⁴6, bb. 44–68)

The long violin melody has the sinuosity of a snake-charmer's incantation.[11] Each of its curves reaches a perfect fourth higher, progressively introducing flat notes into the underlying C mixolydian mode. This is the first of many thematic similarities to Nielsen's incidental music for *Aladdin* (1918–19), and there is also a seed for it in the Fourth Symphony. The theme has ethnic overtones, as a comparison with the basic mode of Armenian folk music[12] and Ravel's *Bolero* makes clear (see Ex. 3).

Motivically Nielsen's theme derives from three sources – the iambic rhythm and initial repetition of the bassoon theme, with the E–F interval expanded to E–G; the minor third of the viola ostinato; and the diminished fifth outline of the 'evil' expansion of this ostinato. The G melodic centre is also carried over and is now reinforced by the second violins' reduplication of the viola ostinato on G and E. Such 'centred' melodies are a Nielsen fingerprint, probably inherited from César

Ex. 3 (a) Fifth Symphony, first movement, fig. 4–³6 (b) *Aladdin*, Act 2, No. 9 (c) Fourth Symphony, first movement, pp. 8–9 (d) Armenian folk–scale (e) Ravel *Bolero*

✔ = slightly flattened untempered degree

Franck, whose music he greatly admired in his youth; the initial repetition is another, probably inherited from Dvořák.[13]

The absence of a bass line was one of the special features of **A1**. Now at last one is supplied, rhythmically complementing the iambs of the melody, in a guise which *looks* like a clear confirmation of F as the tonic (see Ex. 3a). Yet the G–E thematic focus above suggests that the F might be plagal, as was the bassoons' B♭ in section **A1** (fig. 2). Forget the look of the score, stop the passage at any point, and ask whether F or C feels like the tonic. You will hear that C is the stronger contender, even before the bass moves in apparent confirmation. The experience of most listeners is that the introduction of the bass does not 'at last make clear that the key is F'.[14] Rather it maintains an element of ambiguity. We are on an arc between F and C, if anything leaning more towards C at this point. When that inclination is confirmed in the bass, the flat third and seventh (E♭ and B♭) prevent it from over-balancing into unequivocal C major; the final harmony again recalls the open-ended potential-plagal endings of **A1** (see Ex. 3a).

Section A2a (fig. ³6–6, bb. 69–71)

For all the harmonic fluidity of the opening section it was built on an underlying four-bar periodicity (with just one three-bar phrase between the main statement and the liquidation – bb. 21–3). This is replaced in section **A2** by internal extension of the four-bar phrase; the periodicity is 4+4+7+10 bars. In some ways this melody incorporates its own liquidation, as it aspires to grow despite inadequate harmonic fuel. So the pendant is not a liquidation passage, as in section **A1a**, but rather an intensification of the warning of **A1b**, adding the important woodwind timbre to its skirling motion. In this suppressing of the liquidation section the loss of the horn-call motif is significant; indeed the fate of this motif will be crucial to the psychological flux of the movement.

Section A3 (fig. 6–7, bb. 72–84)

The sense of time passing was uncertain from the beginning, and it has taken on a static indifference in **A2**. There is no need to know Nielsen's other music or his aesthetic views to recognise that this is not his idea of a desirable frame of mind. Most of the orchestra is still waiting for something worthwhile to play, and the dynamic level is subdued, having yet to reach beyond a momentary *forte* and *poco forte* at the top of hairpin swells in the 'evil' motif.

How should the returning theme respond to the octave-and-fourth-doubled warning at the end of **A2**? Octave doubling of its own is the first obvious answer. Almost immediately the bass shivers in response. For all the harmonic complexity and uncertainty so far, the music has not been chromatic; it has been juxtaposing and superimposing diatonic elements. Now the bass injects chromatic auxiliaries, as if to challenge whatever harmonic aggregate is formed above it. The melody immediately counters by incorporating similar auxiliaries, elongating them when it moves upwards.

The harmonic focus of this section is still somewhere *between* F and C. This time, however, the upper hand gradually reverts to F by means of subtle changes in the ostinato. Eventually stalemate is reached with a bass descent stuck on the way down to an as yet unknown destination.

Section A3a (fig. 7–8, bb. 84–94)

In **A3** the melody of **A2** was compressed into half its original duration. Now the power of the template asserts itself. Both the contraction of the melody in **A3** and the absence of a liquidation section in **A2** allow Nielsen now to indulge in an extended liquidation. The melodic G's are paralysed into stabbing repeated notes and oscillating fourths; this is an inversion of the tetrachord descent of **A1** and a token of uncertainty of direction which will be greatly expanded in the second movement. The characteristic doubling between oboe and bassoon is something Nielsen probably inherited from Mozart. This texture, and repeated-note themes in general are loosely associated with good humour in Nielsen,[15] but not when placed in a harmonic context such as this. As with the new chromaticisms of **A3**, there is a reciprocal arrangement with the bass, which animates its E♭s with the same staccato note-repetitions, before slipping a further step to D. Again the provenance of the harmony can be traced to *Aladdin* (Ex. 4).

Section A3b (fig. 8–10, bb. 94–109)

For the first time the ostinato transfers to the clarinets, in order to partake the more effectively in the next phase which combines the

Ex. 4 (a) First movement, fig. 7$^{1-6}$ (b) *Aladdin*, No. 4

elements of liquidation (see note 4 above) and warning. If **A3a** liquidated the G tetrachord motif from the opening bassoon melody, **A3b** now liquidates the iambic rhythm and the hairpin dynamic. The warning element is conveyed not by the skirling semiquaver line itself but by insistently repeated appoggiatura harmony.

The C–A element of the ostinato has withdrawn and the G–E element has mutated, almost unnoticed, to G–F. This last is retained through cadential harmonies which seem to lean first towards the upper then towards the lower note, making approach-dominant progressions to C, then plagal cadences in F. The residual Ds from the plagal cadence plant a melodic seed for the following section.

Section A4 (fig. 10–12^3, bb. 109–30)

The next metamorphoses of the main thematic line are foreshadowed by two passages from *Aladdin* – the Prisoners' Dance from Act 2 and the Combat between Good and Evil in Act 4 (Exx. 5b and d). However, nothing in that score could really prepare us for what surrounds the theme. Not that it needs much explaining. The entrance of the side drum ostinato, with its attendant cymbal and triangle, leaves little room for

Ex. 5 (a) Fifth Symphony, first movement, fig. $^{1}11$–11^{5} (b) *Aladdin*, No. 16 (c) Fourth Symphony, first movement, fig. 15^{1-2} (d) *Aladdin*, No. 29

nuances of interpretation. We hardly need to be told that the side drum's rhythm echoes the Fate motif from Tchaikovsky's Fourth, that the unrelenting ostinato recalls Holst's 'Mars, the Bringer of War' from his *Planets* Suite of 1912–13, or that the instrumental colour, metre and ostinato repetition are inherited from Strauss's 'Battle with the Critics' from *Ein Heldenleben* (from the double bar after fig. 49 to fig. 75). But if we find that the side drum is remarkably reminiscent of Ravel's *Bolero* and the 'invasion episode' in the first movement of Shostakovich's 'Leningrad' Symphony, or that the timpani and lower strings recall the crisis point in the first movement of Shostakovich's Fifth (fig. 30), we should remember that Nielsen's Fifth is the earlier by six, nineteen and fifteen years respectively. Direct influence is impossible to prove, but it does seem that Nielsen is here taking part in the creation of a *topos* as much as the drawing on one.

Is this then the real 'evil' motif? Nielsen's commentary suggests not (see Appendix B). But the association with malevolence is reinforced at a deep structural level. Section **A3b** allowed the liquidation withheld in **A2a** to extend over the warning phase, suppressing the 'evil' or warning motif itself, though acknowledging its character in the harmony and tonality. By the beginning of **A4** the minor third ostinato which previously fuelled that warning has shrunk to a major second, with the minor third now heard in a liquidated augmentation. When the cymbal enters with its by now familiar frisson of fear (fig. 9^5) there is no ground for the warning gesture to build on, and the side drum steps into the psychological vacuum. The ostinato has now shrunk a stage further – from minor third to major second to non-pitched rhythm – and the overlap is palpable in the side drum's first three bars. The minor third is then reincarnated in a new ostinato transferred to the bass, which seems intent on dragging the F 'tonic' downwards. The cymbal shiver is reinforced by triangle and the hairpin dynamic is transformed to jagged *forzando* spasms.

The note of anguished intensity infects all aspects of **A4**. The chromatic appoggiaturas introduced in **A3** are further lengthened (the iambic motif now emphasising the *forzandi*), the rising phase of the theme is further contracted, and the quasi-trills of the 'evil' motif prolong the descent phase (see Ex. 5a). The violins build an aggregate based on a diminished rather than minor third,[16] forming a variable eight-step mode. This in turn fluctuates between a diminished seventh 'limbo' and clarification of D minor.

Section A4a (fig. 12^3–14, bb. 130–45)

The quasi-trills carry over into the clarinets' response, which combines liquidation (of the diminished third) and warning, albeit now in an extroverted manner, as well as unobtrusively introducing triplet semi-quavers which will gradually gain in significance. When the flute attempts to match the clarinet's aggression, it does so by adding the stabbing repeated notes to the liquidated diminished thirds, reinstating the melodic focus of G and thereby subtly shifting the harmonic background from a non-committal diminished seventh towards a dominant seventh of C (see Ex. 26).

The long-term significance of this subtle shift will only become apparent two sections further on. The immediate purpose is to underpin the apparently anarchic, writhing quality of the woodwind lines with a controlled harmonic ebb and flow.

Section A5 (fig. 14–15³, bb. 145–58)

The warning phase has now served its purpose and been absorbed into a revised template of thematic and non-thematic, which will underpin the flux of the remainder of the *tempo giusto*.

Section **A4** has been the most strife-torn so far. The 'evil' motif has diversified – into an implacable minor third bass ostinato and a quasi-trill infection of the melody – and the indifferent viola ostinato has given way to a malevolent one on the side drum. The natural response in section **A5** is an attempt to reassert psychological control. The surface symptom of that attempt will be the integration of repeated crotchet Gs into the striving melody. These are taken over from the flute (fig. 13³⁻⁴) and remembered from as far back as section **A3a** (fig. 7–8). It was those repeated notes which deflected the diminished seventh 'limbo' of section **A4** towards a 6–4–3 dominant of C, and their ubiquity in section **A5** reinforces this same trend, compelling the D–F ostinato to contribute to a positive harmonic move. The theme itself forces the previously anarchic clarinet figuration to do something similar.

The whole section represents a gathering of forces. The *molto cantabile* marking for the violins' theme is not only a safeguard against aggressive accentuation; it is also confirmation of a psychological direction towards new achievement and self-assertion. It is the first such expression marking in the score, and it is emblematic of the first positive psychological move. The diminished seventh contour of the theme remains, but the petering out of the theme on a B at fig. 15³ supplies the last ingredient in the re-interpretation of the D–F bass as part of a dominant seventh of C. In **A5** the side drum and its associates have two large hairpin swells, one in the thematic phase, one in the non-thematic which has just begun.

Section A5a (fig. 15³–16, bb. 158–66)

In the meantime the formerly anarchic clarinet and flute are reconstituting the ostinato semiquavers into hyper-energised Janáčekian triplets (compare, for example, the fifth movement of his *Sinfonietta* of 1928). This appropriation of the side drum's characteristic rhythm is a necessary condition for the latter's temporary disappearance. As soon as this new ostinato becomes continuous the side drum fades away, surviving only as a flicker on the tambourine. The repeated Gs in the oboes now sound as beacons, lighting the way to an eventual C major resolution in **A6**.

This completes a process of harmonic overlap which is very pronounced in this and the previous section but which has actually been in operation almost from the beginning of the work. The process will continue, for no sooner has the move to C been made irresistible than the ostinato will de-emphasise C and again sit on the fence. (Ex. 26 summarises the overlap between F-based and C-based tonalities, the musical substance of a flux in character from uncertainty to malevolence to relative recovery.)

Section A6 (fig. 16–18⁶, bb. 166–88)

The *tranquillo* marking confirms what the harmony already tells us – that the long-heralded arrival of C has cleared the air. There is a definite relaxation of tension, and the opening theme returns in something close to its original guise. Simpson observes that '*it is at the same pitch as before, but is now in C*'.[17] However, this is something of an over-simplification. Undoubtedly there is a sense in which the clarification of C represents a step sharpwards on the circle of fifths from the ambivalent F of the opening; this makes it a relative of the upward-fifth tonal progressions of the finales of the Second, Third and Fourth Symphonies, all of which suggest a raising of consciousness. But in this movement the constant intertwining of F and C has been a feature almost from the beginning. We are dealing with a state of flux rather than a straightforward linear progression. Such progression as there has been has pivoted on the intervening ostinato rooted on D; so this is as much a diastematic *fall* to C as it is a functional rise (see Ex. 26).

In any case, how much of the new section is actually 'in C'? The pedal-point admittedly underpins the thematic phase (and it will return with a vengeance in the following section, from fig. 21^6). However, the constant ostinato already leans towards F and strongly counterbalances C when the first horn takes up the F-leaning perfect fourth at fig. 17 (cf. section **A2** at fig. 4).[18] The theme never returns to anything like a C cadence after its first three bars, until a C minor which already sounds seriously undermined seventeen bars further on at fig. 18^5. Meanwhile the pairs of horns and bassoons wander with little purpose around harmonies on a large arc of the circle of fifths (D–G–C–F–B♭). As if to counteract the F-side pull, the horns subsequently try to harmonise the D–C–A ostinato as part of a D dominant seventh. But this attempt, buttressed by the reassuring associations of the horn calls, peters out into chromatic, non-committal thirds. When that petering out happened the first time (at fig. 1^{6-8}) the response was the first gesture of protest in the bassoons. Here the protest is more delayed, but the sensation of a loss of grip is comparable.

If this section is to avoid falling into the same pit as the opening of the work it needs to establish a different direction. This the thematic phase has signally failed to do. The periodic swells to *forzando* on the C pedal, and the persistence of the tambourine shakes, are signs that discontent is never far from the surface. Towards the end of this phase the *forzandos* have infected the thematic line, the tambourine has been joined by the triangle in a horribly reminiscent tremolo, and the viola ostinato has once again lost its focus.

Section A6a (fig. 18^7–19, bb. 189–94)

The bass line now launches a pre-emptive strike. This is the delayed gesture of protest and the first attempt to raise the music by will-power rather than submitting to the pull of gravity. The attempt feels premature, perhaps because inner healing has not yet taken place; and the upward climb is therefore taking place on a psychologically greased slope. All the same, as an initiative it feels defiant, almost heroic. Immediately the side drum and its cohorts counter-attack *fortissimo*. The cymbal and triangle are no longer continuous but join in battle against the determined *forzandi* in the bass line. Harmonic control is virtually in abeyance as the ostinato follows the upwardly mobile bass in distorted quasi–parallel motion. The goal is never made clear.

Section A7 (fig. 19^2–21, bb. 195–212)

In view of the D^7 harmony which had positive implications in the thematic phase of **A6** at fig. 18, perhaps the goal will prove to be G. This would reduplicate the previous large-scale bass move from F to C associated with clarification and new achievement. In that case the sticking-point of G♭, with frustrated stabs at A♭♭, would have precisely the significance Simpson accords it: 'the tonality of this movement rises through fifths, from F to C, and from C to G: the bass has begun its attempts to reach G, but it is foiled at G flat'.[19] A cruder, but equally vital point is that the viola ostinato has not given way to the side drum as before but strives upward and clings on to a strained version of its line, dissonant against the bass throughout section **A7**. Adversity is again in the air, but this time there is a determination to resist.

The bass and the ostinato have made their heroic bid by stepwise rises. The melody now tries to emulate them by shifting the melodic focus from the G of **A6** up to A. The minor third outline of the theme in **A5** is compressed to a diminished third, and the contours are condensed, expressing much the same intensified distress in relation to **A6** as did **A3** in relation to **A2**.

The first phase of the melody clashes with the ostinato, but the second falls in with it, creating an eight-step mode with prominent whole-tone and chromatic segments.

Section A7a (fig. 21–2, bb. 212–25)

The thematic phase of section **A7** has been locked in harmonic limbo – a sign of infection from formerly non-thematic phases. Can the non-thematic phases turn the tables? For a moment it seems possible. The side drum fades away and the oboe takes up the top note of the now silent viola ostinato, making it the middle of an *espressivo con tenerezza* version of the 'evil' motif. This holds out the brief promise of an absorption of a fundamental undermining force of the movement. But the promise is soon broken. The timpani, not heard from for a while, have entered with a B tremolo as a pivot between **A7** and **A7a**. This fulminates away until it provokes violas and cellos to a vice-like re-assertion of a low pedal C, soon to be re-joined by the timpani. The oboe immediately contorts into a grimace and the clarinet needs no further encouragement to reappear in its former anarchic guise, in flux between more or less whole-tone outlines and an A♭ major scale.

Section A7b (fig. 22–4, bb. 225–43)

Another player has meanwhile entered the game. This is the celesta, fixated on pulsing Ds and to be joined in section **A7b** by violins. Here is the germination of a long-dormant idea (cf. flute at fig. 13). Like the previous repeated Gs, this pulsation will eventually have the positive force of dominant preparation and it will provide a melodic focus for the entire second half of the movement. For the time being it is locked into a harmonic time-warp in which remembered fragments of material repeatedly strive to escape the clutches of a whole-tone mode.[20]

At the last moment an arpeggiated chord of A♭ (fig. [2]24, *tranquillo, espressivo*), recalling the clarinet scale of **A7a**, shows that flux is still possible in this time-warp. It is a small but significant step. Again the cymbal provides a frisson of anticipation. Always the harbinger of change, here it seems to hint at a possible new dawn.

Section A8 (fig. 24–5, bb. 243–53)

The re-appearance of pairs of woodwind at the end of section **A7b** is sufficient to encourage another attempt at a version of the main theme. The concluding cello arpeggio (fig. [2]24) prompts the timpani and horn to move to A♭ as a new pedal-foundation. But the signalling repeated Ds remain, as does the triplet descent to a bass C. The theme itself is another paraphrase of the contours of section **A1**, complete with references to the horn call extension. All directional sense is withdrawn, however. The texture is in fact held in the same whole-tone limbo as **A7b**, with harmonic centres descending by major thirds, until finally the memory of the previously positive role of the repeated notes allows the Ds to resolve to an unequivocal G major for the second main phase of the movement.

Section A8a (fig. 25$^{1-15}$, bb. 253–67)

Distant echoes of the tambourine and side drum tattoos fill the non-thematic phase. Flutes and clarinets paraphrase the first modally ambivalent cadence of section **A1**, but now in a C major which is already seriously undermined by the bass. Finally the flute leaves us with an F$\sharp$ which associates loosely with the horn pedal and the stabbing Ds, as an altered dominant of G.

The slowly extinguishing conclusion of this first half of the movement is a device favoured by Nielsen since his Second Symphony (third movement, after letter F). It could be seen as a very crude way of effecting a transition, and certainly it creates a high degree of expectation, which the succeeding music will have to live up to. Fortunately Nielsen has in waiting the finest slow music he ever composed. In so far as it still does not meet expectations, in the sense of engaging stylistically with what has preceded it, Nielsen has strategic reasons for not doing so; and these will lift the ambitions of the symphony onto a higher plane.

The template of thematic and non-thematic sections in the *tempo giusto* gains its power and richness of meaning from the underlying harmonic and tonal forces summarised in Examples 26 and 27.

Section B1 (fig. ^{9}26–^{1}7, bb. 268–83). Self-awareness.

The *adagio*'s breakthrough to G major has been prepared at deep structural levels, as Examples 26 and 27 seek to show. Yet on the surface the new section comes as a shock. The oboe lead-in is extremely difficult to make convincing, poised as it is between two diametrically opposed worlds of experience – paralysis and well-being. The feeling at the beginning of section **B1** is rather like waking up to an unnaturally full state of alertness. Perhaps if conductors were to take Erik Tuxen's injunction *In tempo di Adagio non troppo* (added by him in the 1950 score) more literally than the oboe's *fortissimo* dynamic, and care more for the blend of its last note with the first of the viola theme, there might be less sense of discomfort. But the meshing of emotional gears is still difficult to achieve naturally.

So abrupt is the move that commentators have been inclined either to

Ex. 6 (a) First movement, fig. [9–6]26 (b) *The Mother*, 'My girl is as bright as amber'

censure the composer or even to propose that the first movement would be better thought of as two:

> I consider only the portion of Part 1 preceding the G major *Adagio* as the first movement; the *Adagio*, although it incorporates first-movement material, sounds to me like a new movement (the traditional second movement in a slow tempo).[21]

Christopher Ballantine views the *tempo giusto* as containing exposition and development (though he gives no indication as to the boundary between them) with the *adagio* substituting for a recapitulation, and his view is endorsed by Veijo Murtomäki.[22] Clearly the *adagio* carries the weight of a symphonic slow movement; clearly it is fused with earlier material from the first phase of the movement. But I would prefer to regard that first phase as a unique quasi-strophic design, realising a quasi-programmatic state of mind. It is an anti-movement, in fact, which in the long run is destined to impinge on the 'genuine' world of the *adagio*.

'Suddenly I become aware of myself as a musician' (see Appendix B).

Nielsen's remark seems almost disingenuous. Can it really be as simple as that? Or is this perhaps the sudden awakening of 'the good slumbering in every person, also in me', to which he referred in a letter to his wife of 31 August 1915?[23] In fact there is plenty of reason to take the former statement at something like face value. The suddenness is certainly plain to hear. And the impression of the music starting to speak in the first person may be to do with the fact that the G major theme is the most potent of all Nielsen's 5–1 descents. Jørgen Jensen associates these descents with tokens of nationality and the feminine, summed up in Nielsen's patriotic love-song from his incidental music to *The Mother* (a Helge Rode play celebrating the return of South Jutland to Denmark after the First World War), see Example 6.[24] Becoming aware as a musician has to do with putting to one side the tokens of 'otherness' (the *Aladdin*-derived exotic instruments and modes) and shifting the burden of interest onto evolving harmonic processes. The relatively static, often modal pitch-structures of the *tempo giusto* give way to post-Brahmsian functional tonality; separation of orchestral timbres by family gives way to an integrated texture, with doublings by register instead of by tone-colour.

The newness of this music is striking. Metre, pulse, tonality, functional harmonic language, orchestration, and absence of ostinato, all proclaim it, and the melody's reaching up through degrees of the tonic triad seems to confirm the presence of new constructive effort. Nielsen finally rewards the violas for their previous confinement to mindless oscillation by giving them one of his greatest melodies, and the accented two-note slurs in the cadential phase are one of his most characteristic gestures of reconciliatory warmth (cf. the unmasking scene near the end of his comic opera *Maskarade*).

The melody's flatward drift is another Nielsen fingerprint. It can either transmute the pathos of a tonic minor inflection into pastoral relaxation and warmth, or it can sow the seeds of discontent.[25] The middle of this flatwards drift is held on a harmony of more than local significance (fig. 26, cf. figs. 7, [4]38), before a beautiful variant on a Neapolitan progression returns us to G. A new template has been created, based on harmony as much as on theme and texture. It consists of the reaching-up of the theme, combined with the flatward drift of harmony towards F (around fig. 26), via A♭ ([3–1]27) and potentially beyond, with a last-minute recovery.

What has *not* changed is more subtle but equally important. This concerns not so much the basic motif, although the oboe lead-in encourages us to hear the scalic descent as an outgrowth of the writhing motifs in **A7** and **A8**. More significant is the fact that the inner parts only have two bars of independent movement before giving way to a sinuous doubling in thirds – of the kind associated with the *tempo giusto*'s failure to grow (see **A6**, fig. 18^{3-6}). The subsequent trailing-off is also a disconcerting sign that apparent well-being is less than complete. Above all, the music still has not rid itself of the ball-and-chain of pedal-points, and even the great melody itself is somewhat cautiously attached to its D focus, carried over from **A7** and **A8**. The capacity for freedom of movement has yet to be demonstrated, and there is much to be done if the sense of progress is to be earned rather than merely asserted.

Section B2 (fig. 27–^{1}31, bb. 284–318)

If the *adagio* behaves initially as though nothing had happened, that is precisely the point. The dramatic irony consists partly in the fact that we as listeners know precisely what has happened and that there is unfinished emotional business, partly in that we recognise features which are apparently emotionally neutral but which in the broader context carry negative associations. The new section recognises the fact and sets out to deal with those unresolved problems.

Like section **A1**, **B1** had an underlying four-bar phrase structure. Like **A2**, **B2** will expand this structure from within, this time by contrapuntal rather than melodic means. The promise held out by the new 'self-awareness' theme is seized upon by three melodic voices in an orgy of compositional self-confidence. We can almost the feel the blood beginning to flow through previously numbed veins.

The wandering thirds of the inner parts are soon reduced to a single filling line. The bass stirs itself and confirms the flatward tendency of the theme with a decisive move to the subdominant. This time, however, the melody is more resistant, retaining prominent F♯s, even in the subsequent version of the theme which 'ought' to cadence onto F♮ (violin I, fig. 28^{1-2}). In fact the 'danger' key of F, weakly suggested in **B1**, is bypassed altogether here in a moment of pure contrapuntal ecstasy (fig. 28^{1-2}).[26] The bass line at this point is broken off; when it returns it will generate melodic interest for the first time in the movement (fig. 28$^{2-9}$); it seems that the last ghost of the past has been laid.

The foundations for a truly glorious climax are now in place. The upward-striving arpeggiation of the melody is now borne higher still, eventually culminating in a high G♭=F♯. Underneath it the bass exploits the A♭ region proposed at the end of **B1**, using it as a springboard for an enharmonic pivot, its own subdominant (D♭) becoming supertonic to C♭=B major. The splendour of this key radiates in the three motif-carrying voices singing out the main theme simultaneously, the top part in augmentation, the lower two now adapted to emphasise the triple-time metre. B major represents a peak of achievement in the first movement, and the second movement will attempt (unrealistically as it transpires) to use this peak as a new foundation.

Overcoming the previously pervasive hemiolas is yet another token of the illumination achieved. The thrill of this moment, where so many positive forces meet, is sealed by the new triadic figure in the horns, and it is confirmed by plagal extensions, with a Nielsenesque variant twice contracting the motif so that it bends the flat seventh back into the tonic triad (violin 1, fig. 29$^{4-7}$).

Plagal cadences again lie behind the liquidation phase of this section (fig. 30–1), each bar suggesting a more flatward plagal relationship to B, until the pedal-point is re-interpreted from tonic of B to mediant of G, before shifting down to an A which will function as part of a dominant of the home G major. Meanwhile the treble completes an almost complete stepwise descent over two octaves to an F♯ leading-note.

Section B3 (fig. 31–3, bb. 319–41)

So far, so good. Self-awareness has dawned, along with intimations of a power to grow and absorb, as the basic motif has been heard in close imitation passing through various keys. But all this has happened in an emotional realm which has taken no cognisance of the preceding traumas. What will happen when the opposing states of consciousness confront one another?

The basic plan is a straightforward dialectic. Thesis and antithesis will lead inevitably to conflict and synthesis. Does that make Nielsen's entire project banal? It certainly makes it risky. If the execution only took place at the level of gesture and texture it would be empty, melodramatic in the negative sense. What guards against that is the subtlety of the surface detail and the power of the deeper structural connections.

On the surface nothing initially happens to the 'self-awareness' theme in **B3**, except that it is transposed up an octave and re-scored. But the fact that it is restated in full, ignoring the contrapuntal gains of **B2**, already seems regressive, as does the reduction to *mezzo piano* dynamic. The growth experienced in **B2** has been put aside. It is time for the new state of mind to be tested not against its own inner potential, of which there is now no doubt, but against something external and profoundly inimical.

At the first major–minor darkening (fig. 31[5]) the 'evil' motif enters, centred on D and thus challenging the melodic focus of the 'self-aware-ness' theme on its own ground. As in **B2**, the bass acknowledges the flat-ward drift and shifts from G to C. But in the next bar there is another significant deviation as the theme is infected by the wandering thirds previously confined to middle parts and degenerates into featureless stepwise crotchet movement. It therefore seems natural that the harmony has no power to resist the next flatward step, to the previously avoided F. This betokens total regression, negating every positive har-monic step in the movement so far. The loss of melodic and contrapuntal interest and the harmonic wandering into an established danger area are tokens of an ominous loss of grip.

The theme sings out with fraying pride in this undesirable tonality (fig. 32). Chromatic distortions attempt to bend it out of trouble as the harmonic template of **B1** and **B2** is called up, with A♭ twice leading the way forward, the first time towards the positive B, the second time with its familiar neapolitan approach role back to the dominant of G.

Section B3a (fig. 33–[1]7, bb. 341–76)

The next phase draws on both templates in the movement. In accordance with the *adagio*'s harmonic template the A♭ region has arrived at the dominant of G. But this dominant is now vastly expanded as a pedal-point on the timpani, lasting 36 bars before resolution to the tonic is granted. This is where the liquidation and warning elements of the *tempo giusto* template come into play, producing an extended passage of harmonic stalemate. D is of course the same timpani pedal-note as underpinned the first appearance of the side drum in section **A3**, a fact which is surely not coincidental either to the latter's re-emergence or to the decisiveness of its defeat when the pedal note's long fuse finally detonates in a colossal perfect cadence. The music above and around this pedal-point includes the famous side drum cadenza where the player is instructed to 'improvise as though at all costs to disturb the music'.[27] This 36-bar confrontation intensifies in progressive steps:

(1) The D-centred 'evil' motif on the woodwind is reduplicated in the strings, centring on C. These are the dominants of the two main tonal protagonists of the movement – the 'vegetative' F and the 'self-aware' G. At the same time the passage brings to horrible fruition the seed planted in the first two dyads of the opening bassoon theme.

(2) The 'self-awareness' motif is repeated in stepwise rising sequence until it hits a crunch dissonance on A♭ (fig. 34). This precipitates the crisis, touching off the venomous return of the side drum – *diabolus ex machina* in its original four-four metre but now faster[28] – while the first trumpet and trombone play a parody of the triumphant augmentation of the theme in **B2**. Previously the side drum had been confined to its original rhythm, as a symbol of unchanging negativity. Now, rather like the 'self-awareness' G major theme in **B2**, it diversifies and colonises (rhythms rather than keys). The next stage for the side drum is a notated, then free cadenza.

(3) The brass's chorale-like harmonies explore a tonal arc of B♭–E♭–A♭, deflecting finally to F (fig. 34–5), thus giving a retrograde version of the harmonic template of the *adagio*.

(4) The F major entry of the 'self-awareness' theme is on four unison horns, an ironic reference, perhaps, to the heroic climax of Strauss's *Don Juan* (fig. Y). It is reinforced by third trombone and tuba on a pedal C. In response, the second and third trumpets attack repeated Ds, using the tattoo rhythm which the frenzied side drum has by now abandoned. Thus the balance of forces has been retained within a general intensification. For a while this apparent stalemate continues, with the horn and trombone thirds emphasising G minor and F minor scale segments in turn (fig. 35–6). The D-centred tattoos become more insistent, but the C-centred 'evil' motifs rise through octaves to meet them. Meanwhile the A♭ 'crunch-harmony' has returned (fig. 36), and finally its dominant draws the C bass chromatically up to D, via a German Sixth approach

chord. This is the decisive breaking of the stalemate which sets up the engulfing perfect cadence in G.

Section B4 (fig. 37–9³, bb. 377–400)

The 'evil' motif, the side drum and the fatal tonality of F have all been swallowed up by the cadence. The triumph is now sealed in ways more subtle than the *fff* dynamic and tutti scoring. The 'self-awareness' motif is harmonised by a reconciliation of the directionless parallel thirds and the long-lost horn calls, while the 'evil' motif is transformed into energetic rushings in the lower strings, which first absorb the dominant-to-F version of the motif then engulf it in pure G major. Both the 'self-aware-ness' motif and the rushing bass are then massively augmented. The former has already been adapted at the beginning of **B4** to fall to the supertonic rather the tonic, its open-endedness setting up repeated perfect cadences. The third of these cadences is now massively extended so as to accommodate a striding G major scale balanced by a final acknowledgement of the dominant-to-F version of the 'evil' motif. This definitive release of the bass from its fixation on pedal-points is another vital token of psychological progress. The peak sonority here refers back to what was an anxiously frozen aggregate in **A3a** and a near-capitula-tion to F in **B1a** (fig. 37⁹, cf. figs. 7, 26²), transcending a G/F verticalisa-tion in a final confirmatory perfect cadence.

All that remains is for the glorious climax to relax through liquidated echoes of the cadence and a final gesture of acquiescence from the side drum. The G⁷ version of the 'evil' motif is recalled by the bassoons and flutes, then given the most poetic transformation of all in the clarinet cadenza. This simultaneously assuages the evil character of the motif and the inimical timbre of the solo clarinet; and its extension reconciles the thematicised versions of the motif as remembered from **A2–5** (in the cadenza's diminished seventh ascent) and the movement's pinnacle of hope in **B3** (in the further extension of the diminished seventh to a criti-cal high-point of C♭ [=B]).

Simpson's metaphor of the last post over a battlefield is difficult to resist.[29] Indeed Nielsen originally marked the clarinet recitative 'langt i Baggrunden' [far in the background]; Erik Tuxen's 1950 revised score substitutes 'quasi molto lontano'. Perhaps the practicalities of having the clarinet literally off-stage are insuperable. But the side drum (originally 'i Baggrunden'; in the 1950 score 'molto lontano') is usually played off-stage, to symbolise its banishment. An element of recalcitrance remains in its rhythmic variety as it marches off looking for new arenas to terrorise.

The outline harmonic structure of Sections **B1–4** is summarised in Example 28. It is now also possible to step back and express the entire tonal drama of this colossal first movement as a deeper middleground structure in neo-Schenkerian terms (for a brief explanation of Heinrich Schenker's theory of tonal music, see the preamble to Appendix C); and if the 'Vegetativ' of the *tempo giusto* is viewed as essentially unreal, as preparatory to 'self-awareness', and yet crucial to its unfolding, a background structure could even be proposed (Ex. 29). Such an apparently idiosyncratic presentation, with the entire *tempo giusto* first half of the movement lying outside the framework of the fundamental structure, may seem far-fetched and arcane. But it corresponds to the music's fundamental oppositions of passive/active, unreal/real, in which 'self-awareness as a musician' only dawns in the *adagio*. And it finds some surprising, if informal, corroboration in Povl Hamburger's description of the form as a 'toccata with improvisatory-ornamental introduction', if I am correct in reading his 'introduction' as denoting the entire *tempo giusto* section.[30]

The reader who has had the forbearance to follow thus far and to tackle the summaries in Appendix C may not take kindly to being told that all this only represents one way of viewing the structure. But when a harmonic language is as rich in ambiguity as Nielsen's it would be absurd to lay claim to definitive understanding, just as no conductor should lay claim to the definitive interpretation in performance. What needs no apology, I believe, is the attempt to engage at this level of detail with a musical composition of genius.

In the middle of his work on the first movement Nielsen wrote to the Swedish critic Julius Rabe, crucially modifying the motto of 'The Inextinguishable':

> [Music] *is* life or it *is* death. The other arts represent life. Music also does
> that after its fashion – in another way – but at the same time it is alive itself

and moves, and therefore the strength of its effect should be precisely double that of the other arts *at the moment [of communication]* [*i Øjeblikket* – original emphases], and that is indeed the case, of course provided that the right conditions (appreciation, understanding etc.) are present.[31]

Accounting for this double-strength effect is a daunting challenge. Step-by-step observation of the textures and thematic characters of the music is not a bad start, and drawing analogies with life or the other arts is a natural extension.[32] But if we find Nielsen's music up to the task of embodying such huge ethical issues, that is because every stage in its unfolding drama is absorbed into the hierarchic language of tonal harmony. This is the medium through which the music's life and motion can be most fully observed, which is the point of the reductive examples in Appendix C and of their specialised notation.

3

The second movement: alert forces

In an interview published at the time of the Fifth Symphony's first per-formance, Nielsen mentioned that he had been preoccupied with the question of the four-movement symphonic mould.[1] It was an issue he had already addressed in the Violin Concerto (FS61, 1911), each of whose two buoyant movements is prefaced by an extended introverted prelude. And he would return to it throughout the 1920s, not least in the two-movement flute concerto.[2] His explorations place him alongside Sibelius as one of the most intrepid seekers for new patterns of sym-phonic construction.

Building on remarks from Nielsen's own lectures, Danish scholars see this search in terms of a gradual move from an architectonic to an organic view of large-scale form, that is, from taking the four-movement mould as a given to allowing the drama of the musical materials themselves to gen-erate a unique large-scale form.[3] In the case of the Fifth Symphony, however, Per Nørgård is surely right to refine this idea by identifying a confrontation between the principles of organic growth and absolute contrast.[4] The *tempo giusto* clearly disregards the traditional sonata-form first movement; but the remainder of the symphony takes into account the demands of the four-movement scheme, working out a tension between the organic and architectonic principles. Within the first movement the dichotomy between the *tempo giusto* and the *adagio* is so severe that at least one serious commentator has suggested it would be better to call them two separate movements (see chapter 2 above, p. 35). Yet their interdepen-dence at dramatic and thematic levels is such that they demand to be con-sidered as a single unit, a fusion of an unprecedentedly non-progressive 'first movement' and an unprecedentedly strife-torn 'slow movement'. This would then suggest the need for the kind of balancing movement Nielsen in fact undertakes – a fusion of scherzo and finale.

The second movement's unique design is ultimately dictated by a psychological scenario, though not one that Nielsen himself ever disclosed, even to the limited extent he did with his first movement. It is in the manner of a sequel, in which the 'first person' subject matter of the first movement is replaced, initially at least, by a less individualistic manner. Robert Simpson effectively catches the tone of the opening: 'From the ashes and ruins left by the conflict [of the first movement] rise the regenerative energies of man.'[5]

The way in which this scenario is enacted musically can be followed in much more detail than was possible for Simpson in his life-and-works study, and with different nuances. It is worth the effort, for this finale is one of the most masterly in symphonic history in its compositional embodiment of 'big issues'. If it does not always seem so in performance, that can often be put down to simple mismanagement of the main tempo. *Allegro*, dotted minim = 72–6, is a marking ignored at a conductor's peril (see chapter 4 below). Admittedly it is *observed* only at the orchestra's peril (especially from fig. 59, where the strings have been known to plead for the conductor to beat three in a bar),[6] and it is none too easy to cope with the change from triplets to straight quavers at the *un poco più mosso* at fig. 64 and the two-stage *accelerando* into the *presto* fugue (fig. 70–1). But a safe tempo for this long opening section (section A in the analysis which follows) is surely an abuse of its character and dramaturgy. This is an intricately composed-out collapse, and as that fact gradually becomes apparent, so a sense of desperation becomes gradually more palpable. Complacency in the tempo would be fatal.

Section A1 (opening–fig. 40[5], bb. 1–23). Assertion; Drift.

'I would like the listener as it were to brace himself and become alert and healthy, even amidst the greatest ecstasy.'[7] Here we have, twenty years later, the musical translation of Nielsen's statement. The bracing tone of the opening needs little discussion. This is the last and greatest of Nielsen's athletic triple-time movements. Faster than the triple-time first movements of the great Third Symphonies – Beethoven's 'Eroica', Schumann's 'Rhenish', Nielsen's 'Espansiva' (and Brahms's Third, which is actually notated in six-four, though for much of its length it feels as if in a fast three) – faster also than the finale of 'The Inextinguishable' (marked dotted minim = 63), it nevertheless shares many of their musical features. The triadic thematic outlines, plentiful hemiolas and cross-accentuations, to which Nielsen adds a rapid upward-striving contour echoing that of the *adagio*'s 'self-awareness' theme, all have connotations of energy and well-being.[8]

The finale of 'The Inextinguishable' confronted its positive opening statement with emblems of destruction, in the shape of two sets of dinning timpani. The Fifth Symphony, however, has already had its pitched battle between Good and Evil. What is left? The answer is the disheartening complications which assail the reconstruction process and provoke a despair as real as that of the first movement. And just as the first movement's *adagio* theme carried unobtrusive reminders of unfinished business, so the opening of the second movement is not so securely founded as it might appear. It too carries with it the seeds of its own downfall.

One of these seeds is intervallic. It might seem that the emphasis on perfect fourths was the ideal complement to the first movement's pervasive seconds and minor thirds. Nielsen inherited from the ancient Greeks a belief in the ethical quality of intervals, and the falling fourth was a stereotype he deplored, at least at certain stages in his life.[9] In fact there were some prominent fourths in the first movement, sparingly used but generally associated with a tonal leaning towards the fatal key of F (sections **A2** and **A6**, fig. 4–5, 17^{1-4}) and with loss of momentum (section **A3a**, fig. 7–8). Such associations may at first seem far removed from the positive thinking of the *allegro*, but they will return to haunt it.

With unobtrusive pathos the clarinet recitative at the end of the first movement arched upwards to a $C\flat/B\natural$. That was also the key of the most hopeful climax of the movement and it is now the key in which the second movement begins. Or is it? Nielsen himself had problems deciding on a key signature for the second movement, just as he did for the first. At the bottom of the first page of his draft score he wrote and crossed out 'E dur fortegn? A dur?' [E major key signature? A major?]. He settled on three sharps – the key signature given in the fair copy and in the 1926 printed score, but omitted by the editors of the 1950 revision. This three-sharps signature is in place all the way to the F minor *presto* fugato – a startling discovery for anyone unfamiliar with the earlier score. It need not be taken to indicate that Nielsen felt that the opening was 'in

Ex. 7 (a) Second movement, bb. 1–6 (b) *Helios* Overture, bb. 5–12

A major', of course; the key signature could just as well have been a matter of convenience. But it offers corroboration for the feeling that the apparent security of the apparent B major is already compromised by the trilled E pedal in flutes, clarinets and violas (see Ex. 7). Nielsen's opening paragraphs often have an in-built flatwards tendency; this follows the natural implications of his favourite modal flat seventh, and it thereby motivates exertions of will-power to recover the tonic. But it has never before appeared in such an impacted guise. This opening runs true to form in eventually leading flatwards to a repeated, accented E^7 chord (fig. 40$^{1-4}$), which will lead to further flatwards progression in section **A1a**.

But things are a little more complicated than that. The semitone motif (**y**) in the middle of the texture (see Ex. 7) pulls the melody towards the tonic minor (bb. 7–10), immediately to be followed by eight bars of arpeggiation of F$_\sharp$ minor. Not only does the pedal E remind us of earlier disastrous pedal points, but the other notes of the main motif (**x**) are also retained as quasi-ostinatos or harmonic pivots, so that the whole section has a unified harmonic colour (see Exx. 7, 11, 12, 13). The superimposition of motifs gives each beat competing emphasis, like a turbulent version of the 'sunrise' opening of the *Helios* Overture (see Ex. 7). We have been plunged *in medias res*.

The shift of harmonic emphasis from one note to another within a constant aggregate recalls section **A3b** in the first movement (fig. 8–10, the tense passage just before the entry of the side drum). This is the subtlest indication of a residual tension needing to be worked out. It gives the aspiring tone of the thematic surface an underlying instability.

The rising scale of b. 19 does not spark off a restatement (as does its historical model, bb. 35–6 of Beethoven's 'Eroica', first movement). If it did, that restatement would presumably have to be in the subdominant, E. Instead the accented quavers hammer away on an E^7 chord which is conventionally resolved via a balancing downward scale into A at the beginning of **A1a**. At this point the quavers feel like a welcome excess of energy, and the move to A major is a welcome harmonic clarification. But once again Nielsen is setting up the pattern for a longer-term process whose ramifications will be far from welcome. The extending sub-sections in the finale will be more thematically charged (at least initially) than their first-movement counterparts, but the so-promising quavers will be the agent which transforms that charge into something horribly reminiscent of the non-thematic sections of the first movement. The reversal of character reflects the insidiousness of the flatwards drift already implanted in the opening bars. Pride comes before a fall, and the opening gambit just examined will be shown to have been too confident for its own good.

The tonal orientation of section **A1** can now be shown as follows (Ex. 8). As in the early stages of the first movement, the distinctive quality of Nielsen's harmony – its localised asperity and its mid-term mobility and structural force – arises from its dwelling on arcs of the circle of fifths, rather than moving from point to point.

Section A1a (fig. 40^5–3, bb. 23–46). Jolts.

The signs of conflicting interests are sharpened in the continuation. Here the z motif from the bass of **A1** (see Ex. 7) is elevated to principal thematic status, wherein it explores flatward-leaning modal regions within A major. The harmony is schizophrenic, however. At first (fig. 40^5–^{2}41) its flatward instincts are resisted by the hard-held pedal B in the bassoons, as if unwilling to grant the effacing of the initial tonic of the movement and attempting to divert the centre of gravity back sharp-

Ex. 8 Second movement, section A1

wards; variations on this phenomenon will be a recurrent token of resistance to the inevitable flatwards collapse of section **A**. Then the bassoons shift to C, while the harmony in the horns explores still flatter regions, with the result that an outcome on D^7 is a compromise, the best that can be achieved in the circumstances (fig. 41^{1-7}).

At this point (fig. $^2 42$) there is a short-circuit across the circle of fifths. This is structurally a far more crucial event than at first appears. The D^7 chord seems to be a nerve-centre, a touchstone for the psychological health of the music. To let the flatward drift continue beyond this point is a prospect not yet to be contemplated. Here the drift is contradicted by a $D\flat (=C\sharp)$ major scale, a short-circuit in the sense that it is a jump from the flat side to the sharp side of B, which could then re-instate the tonic via the already established flatward drift. But this would be too easy, and another short-circuit takes us to $B\flat$, which again immediately inclines flatwards.

These jolting attempts to reject the flatward drift may be represented as follows (Ex. 9).

Section A1b (fig. 43–5, bb. 46–64). Abrasions, fall.

Progress is now proving problematical. In the second developmental extension of **A1**, variants of the x motif apparently seek to 'colonise' harmonic fields by close imitation, as did the G major theme of the first movement's *adagio*. At the same time the y motif reappears to agitate the quaver motion and soon itself mutates to a whole tone (from fig. 44). The harmonic near-confusion conceals a twofold flatwards drift – from the initial $B\flat$, by whole-tone steps down to D (expressed in a bass-line slippage that will also be significant in section **A2a**), and from B (staking its claim in near-bitonal opposition, as in **A1a**) by circle-of-fifths steps to the same D destination (Ex. 10). This completes a section which moves

49

Ex. 9 Second movement, section A1a

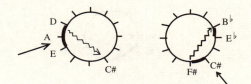

Ex. 10 Second movement, section A1b

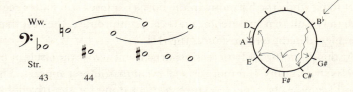

from thematic impacting (at the opening of the movement) to harmonic impacting.

Section A2 (fig. 45–7⁴, bb. 64–96). Drift; mild jolt.

Once again D has been touched on and emphasised as a stage in a danger-ous flatwards drift. This time it is not decisively rejected but gently dealt with as a plagal cadence to A. At this point the air clears and a new-sounding theme is heard, the first from a solo instrument in the move-ment (oboe, *mp cantabile*), and with no competing bass movement. The theme's relationship to the x motif is made explicit in the tailpiece, and it has the same 2+4–bar phrase-structure as the beginning of **A1** (see Ex. 7). Its derivation from the y motif is more subtle (see Ex. 11).

The harmonic support of this theme is an explicit statement of the underlying harmony of **A1** (see Ex. 7), and it receives an explicit resolu-tion (into A major) that the near-tonic sonority of **A1** never had, momen-tarily relaxing harmonic tension for the first time. Meanwhile the arching contours of the theme are pacified into an accompanying arpeg-giation (see Ex. 11). The consequent 8–bar phrase introduces a note of concern with an intervallically contracted version of the new motif, a diminished seventh harmony and a D pedal, plagal to the new key –

Ex. 11 (a) Second movement, fig. 45[1-6] (b) derivation of A2 motif from A1, A1b

uneasy shades of the first movement (cf. fig. 9). An open-ended period structure[10] is completed by a repetition of the first phrase with descant (an attempt to defuse the scalic quaver continuation, just as the new theme itself attempts to pacify the first theme) and by a concluding phrase controlled by minor third ascents in the treble and a diminished seventh pivot (see Ex. 12), balancing the two 6-bar shortened phrases by an extension to 12 bars (6+8+6+12).

Section A2a (fig. 47[4]–[1]9, bb. 96–115). Fall.

The diminished seventh enables an uneasy sharpwards recovery to an E harmonic focus to take place. But this time the resolution is withheld, and during the canonic liquidation of the **A2** motif the bass slips down by whole-tones (cf. **A1b**, fig. 44–5), now associating repeated quavers with the fall and further transmuting the accompaniment crotchets into repeated up-bow staccatos. Once again the pull is towards D[7] (cf. fig. [2]42, [4ff]45) (see Ex. 13). Each of these features will prove germane to the long collapse of section **A3a–e**.

Section A3 (fig. 49–[4]52, bb. 116–50). Exhilaration; warning.

The whole-bar striding chords which follow, reminiscent of the Chaconne finale of Brahms's Fourth Symphony, are immensely invigorat-

Ex. 12 Second movement, section A2

Ex. 13 Second movement, section A2a

ing. Their apparently unfettered energy seems to bear out Nielsen's remark that for him the horizontal was equated with subjectivity, while harmony was essential to establish objectivity.[11] But the deeper meaning of this passage lies in the context established, and it is rather more equivocal.

Two patterns have emerged so far, both of them worrying – the flat-ward drift from B as far as D, and the de-thematicising of motifs into quaver scales and repeated staccato crotchets. Section **A3** bows to one of these trends and attempts, with some initial success, to refute the other. Its theme makes a virtue out of the repeated notes from **A2a** (compare the hopeful striving G crotchets in the first movement, section **A5** from fig. 14) and develops the pattern of **A2** in placing the x motif at the end of the basic 6-bar phrase (4+2, rather than the 2+4 of the previous main themes). Having established these positive features, the theme gains confidence by embracing harmonies not governed by the circle of fifths, by developing more polyphonic interchange, by stretching its concluding motif to cover an octave, and by planting sturdy crotchet scales within secure diatonic harmony. There are even signs of the quavers themselves being turned to positive force (from fig. [5]51), and the downplaying of fourths in both melody and harmony seems to suggest a determination to sail against the prevailing winds.

However, positive actions can be over-ridden by the arena in which they take place. What the optimistic surface of the music conceals is that the Rubicon of D has finally been crossed. Nielsen has allowed the music to slip a further step flatwards to G, which is accepted as a temporary tonic and reconfirmed by the first full cadences of the section. G represents a further whole-tone descent in the initiation of sub-sections (**A1** begins in B, **A2** in A, now **A3** apparently in G); the next step will be the most complex and the most catastrophic – the fall to F for the *presto* fugue.

So the apparent optimism and well-being of the Brahmsian theme are based on a sell-out. When G major harmony later moves round the circle of fifths towards E♭ a warning is sounded (fig. 51) with dissonant appoggiaturas to the dominant, involving motif **y**, the energy-draining quaver scales, and finally an imperfect cadence in E♭ *minor*. Ex. 14 shows this passage and a circle-of-fifths representation of the entire **A3** sub-section.[12]

Section A3a (fig. [4]52–[1]7, bb. 150–215). Attempted recovery; impending anarchy.

The balance of power, conveyed by the tonal orientation, has dramatically shifted, and the false-positive aspects of the surface allow psychological space for this change to become gradually manifest. The unison string quavers which fulminate away under the following 100 bars of music are by no means arbitrary, but their sense of direction is so intermittent as to give them a decidedly anarchic feel. The scoring for the strings as a block is in itself a strong reminder of the conflict-torn paragraphs of the first movement; it is also a continuation from the bitonal grinding of **A1b** which the intervening music has tried to forget. In

Ex. 14 Second movement, fig. ^{1}51–51^9, section A3

addition the repeated-quaver feature which was associated with loss of direction in **A1** is soon to come out into the open.

How should we understand the horns' concert-pitch C♭ (B♮ in the 1926 score)? Obviously it comes gesturally out of the warning acciaccaturas – see Example 14. Does it also represent another attempt to hold onto the 'home' key despite the prevailing flatwards drift? Apparently yes, because for a while the rushing quavers stabilise on F♯ and D♯, which flute and bassoon interpret as part of B major with the **A2** theme. Any positive force this holding-on might have is called into question, however, by the texture – the strings' central minor third with melody above and below is a thinly disguised reminder of the vegetating music at the opening of the first movement (sections **A1a**, **A1b**, **A2** etc.).

The controlling force within the quavers is partly motivic. It crystallises around variants of the three-note descent of the **A2** motif, which itself is undergoing variation above them. The control is partly harmonic too, in that the quavers almost always contrive to form seventh chords with the triadic harmonisation of the **A2** motif (see fig. 54 to 57, wherever the strings have repeated notes). The rise and fall of the quavers also helps to define the ebb and flow of the sub-section, especially in passages where they are heard independently of the **A2** motif. In such cases their direction is upward on the first two occasions (fig. ^{4}52–52, 52$^{12–15}$), then static (fig. 53$^{8–12}$), then downward for the last two occasions (fig. 54$^{7–11}$, 55$^{6–9}$). The harmonised **A2** motifs in the woodwind fall into two descending sequences, the second more dissonant and culminating in further 'warning' *forzando* dissonances (fig. 56^{6}–57). The C$\sharp^7$ chord favoured as a resting-place is carried over into **A3b**.

Section A3b (fig. 57–9, bb. 216–50). Enmeshed.

We are now all at sea. Tuba and bassoons lurch in with the original **x** motif, yet again trying to salvage B major from the chaos above it. In two upward-striving waves the attempt at B is thrown off towards axially related keys – first A♭ at fig. 57$^{10–16}$, then F with superimposed D major at fig. ^{4}59–59. This is the first time that the fatal key of F has been significantly mooted in this movement, but not the first time that D has been a punctuating element with negative connotations.

Within this loose framework all is uncertainty. The fast harmonic rhythm and equivocal direction of the **A2** motif in the previous sub-section are taken over in the woodwind and horns, but with no thematic content, merely a complementary rhythm to the **x** motif, along with rushing quavers which are even more anarchic than before. Rarely do all three elements of the texture coalesce harmonically (the E♭ minor of fig. 57$^{8–9}$ and the B major of fig. ^{1}58–58^2 are close to being exceptions; and if the strings are written in flats, as they were in the original score, the A♭ orientation of fig. 57$^{10–16}$ becomes clearer to the eye). This sub-section is frantically looking for a way forward but only succeeds in enmeshing itself more thoroughly.

Section A3c (fig. 59–^{1}64, bb. 250–302). Assertion; defiance.

One hundred bars of unison quavers have got the strings nowhere. Now they make a defiant bid to energise the sapping force, attacking with triplet quavers, rising through an arpeggiation of A♭ major (thus continuing the axial-harmony tendency of **A3b**) and eventually holding aloft 30 bars of a piercing high B – the fifth and last attempt to regain this promised land. Underneath this the **x** motif is still searching for a way ahead, trying D and C♯ in close imitation and settling on horn calls in D, which as before combine positive surface and negative foundation; the horn calls here show themselves to be as much part of the problem as of the solution.

The x motif is played in a hopeful E major, and the horn calls try to regain the A2 motif in F♯ minor, answered by woodwind in C♯ minor, all under the piercing high B in the violins. Each note of the referential harmony of A1 is being separately explored, even more systematically than at the beginning of the movement. But the thematic rhythm is lost and non-differentiation mounts as the horn call is gradually dispersed in parallel thirds, recalling loss-of-direction passages in the first movement and falling through a disturbing touch of F major at fig. 62[6–8].

At each stage in the harmonic process the strings voice their protest with *ffz* eruptions (effectively reinforced by timpani in Tuxen's revised score).[13] The descent of the strings' triplets is through a decorated arpeggiation of F♯ minor; again the first *ffz* breaks the pattern, setting up a circle-of-fifths fall and finally a settling back to the D major the sub-section was trying so hard to escape from in the first place.

Section A3d (fig. 64–7, bb. 303–50). Liquidation.

It is characteristic of the entire *allegro* that the non-thematic 'buffer' sub-sections are longer then the thematic ones, and the more such buffers accumulate in A3 the more a sense of panic grows that constructive statement of any kind will be impossible to restore. The string triplets of A3c were a last desperate bid to restore B as tonic – a manic energising of the unison quavers which had been choking the momentum of the music. Now the strings return to quavers, but with a slight increase in tempo (an extremely difficult change to negotiate in performance, but one that is crucial in the lemming-like onrush toward the F minor fugue). Unlike their appearance in A3a and A3b, however, they strongly reinforce a pitch-centre – the equivocal D.

There is now yet another attempt to state the A2 theme, at a level which would suggest a tonic G, but harmonised so as to cadence repeatedly on D. A fixation develops with the D triad, until all that can be done is to repeat it in staccato crotchets horribly reminiscent of the loss-of-direction phases of the first movement (see fig. 21–5[15]). Underneath this a subtle evolution takes place in the repeated quavers. They gradually introduce flat inflections – E♭, A♭, B♭, C♮, F♮, G♭, F♭ – until a region of A♭ as dominant of D♭ minor (!) is reached, a tritone away from the D/G suggested at the outset of the sub-section. Meanwhile the rushing quavers have been slowed to quadruplets, converging rhythmically on the D major crotchets.

Section A3e (fig. 67–[1]71, bb. 350–409). Limbo.

For the first time in the movement, in fact for the first time in the whole symphony, there is a virtual absence of rhythmic differentiation between layers; and the only melodic differentiation is a forlorn perfect fourth, a pale shadow of its formerly thrusting self. Woodwind and strings exchange tritonally-opposed repeated-note ciphers on the dominants of G and D♭, while the harmony drifts sharpwards (N.B.!) from D♭ towards F (Ex. 15).

Ex. 15 Second movement, section A3e

Simpson hears the alternation of A♭ and D as 'contradictory keys', with F as the 'mean'.[14] But the harmony has by now ceased to have anything to do with D and is engaged in a sharpwards pull to F – significant that the only extended sharpwards pull encountered so far in this movement is involved in establishing an inimical key.[15] Finally the dominant of F is left unchallenged, and a combined *diminuendo* and *accelerando* tips us into the next phase of the movement, rather as the first movement's *tempo giusto* petered out with unresolved tritones and a glimmer of dominant preparation (see fig. 25[1–15]).

The last two subsections have become less eventful, less dense, but at the same time more controlled than their precursors. The trouble is that the control has become associated with the reverse of well-being, and the decrease in eventfulness suggests impotence.

In fact the *allegro* as a whole is an astonishing example of a compositionally controlled collapse. Thematically and texturally the loss of direction is readily apparent. Tonally it is more subtle, since the collapse is registered both diastematically **and** functionally – a descent from B to A to G to F at the head of each successive section, and a flat-wards progression through the intervening steps on the circle of fifths. Both aspects appear also in microcosm, resisted on occasions by major-third axes, circle-of-fifths ascents, and attempts to reinstate the initial B major by plucking it out of thin air. The intricate tonal and harmonic processes of this first phase of the finale are represented in Example 30.

It is bad enough when innocence is assailed and contorted by evil, as in the first movement's *tempo giusto*. It is bad enough when that evil returns to assault a determined assertion of personality and an attempt to grow, as in the *adagio*. The composed collapse of the second movement's *allegro* might then seem to be going over the same ground. In fact it is a further intensification, despite, or rather because of, the absence of overt evil.

The key to the downfall of the side drum in the first movement *adagio* was that it was given free rein, the implacable menace of its rhythmic leit-motif being allowed to diversify and eventually to boil over into unre-strained anarchy and thereby exhaust itself. All the positive 'self-awareness' force needed to do in these circumstances was to stand firm and contain the onslaught, to ride out the storm. In the second movement the key to the crisis experienced is similar, except that this time it is the positive force which burns itself out. Malevolence sits quietly by until it can move unopposed into the driving-seat. If anything the crisis is therefore even deeper than that of the first movement.

In many ways the technical realisation of this collapse is also predi-cated on the early stages of the *adagio*. A positive (major-mode, upward-striving) theme shows a worrying tendency to drift flatwards; it attempts to counteract the tendency, colonising the orchestral texture (by close imitation) and other tonalities. Crucially, however, the undermining process is more drastic than in the *adagio* and the interim achievements more superficial. And since the starting-point is more hopeful, there is a greater distance to fall psychologically. It is tempting to associate all this with the crisis in Nielsen's marriage, although there is no external evi-dence other than chronology to support the connection. Whatever the background circumstances or intentions, however, Nielsen has thoroughly subsumed them in the language of music, so that if anything the converse aplies – that in examining the details of this musical language we may also be examining an aspect of the composer's inner life.

The second movement has taken up the 'crowning-glory' key of the first movement – B major – which is also maximally removed from the fateful F on the circle of fifths. The achievements of section A on this basis are entirely in the thematic realm, with two further themes sparked off whose state of well-being is confirmed in their triadic tonal clarification, however temporary. By contrast the achievement in the first movement's G major 'self-awareness' phase was a harmonic one – in the music's thinking its way through to the harmonic sharp side, especially in section B2. In the second movement all is far from well with each of the three main themes harmonically. The undermining of the opening theme takes two forms. First is an extended fall around the circle of fifths, particularly a three-step fall from B through E and A to D, but threatening the full six-step collapse to F; second is the descent into a non-thematicism reminiscent of the 'vegetating' of the *tempo giusto*. The x motif loses its upward-driving optimism, and the stepwise ascent it generates at its first appearance (see Ex. 7) is never heard from again. Similarly the A2 motif soon falls into liquidating repetitions and never regains the harmonic innocence and linear clarity it first enjoyed, while the intervallic distortion in its consequent phrase will become the norm in A3a and A3b rather than the exception. Again the repeated notes of the section A3 theme lose their harmonic clarity after being assailed by dissonant *acciaccaturas*, returning only as anxious staccatos in almost bitonal contexts, which provides yet another disturbing reminder of the first movement's 'vegetating'. Miserably, the horn calls associated with triumph in the first movement are here forced to partake in the liquidating process which is the musical counterpart of a draining away of stable identity.

Section B (fig. 71–92, bb. 410–679). The 'mad' fugue.

The stage is set. The collapse is complete. The staccato repeated notes, undifferentiated rhythmically or melodically, peter out on the lowest string of the violas, one of the hollowest timbres available to a composer.

Ex. 16 (a) Second movement, fig. 71$^{1-8}$ (b) Dukas, *The Sorcerer's Apprentice*

The fatal key of F has been reached. None of the diversionary tactics of section **A** has worked. F has even dealt the home key of B the indignity of finding sharpwards progressions to set itself up, precisely the affirmation never granted to the 'home' key of B. The final approach-dominant preparation is sufficient to implant F.

'Mere anarchy is loosed upon the world.' Given the experience of the first movement, that might well be the fear. And what ensues largely fulfils the expectation. Yet this is, at least to start with, a deceptively self-possessed anarchy, and all the more destructive for that. Unlike the comparable end of the first movement's *allegro giusto*, the repeated notes which usher in the new section are still metrically charged. The triple-time *presto* has been reached by a two-phase acceleration and its unnaturally driven tempo will be held, along with the F minor tonality, for the full 269-bar duration of this section.

Despite the various historical backgrounds already cited, pretty well everything about Nielsen's Fifth is *sui generis*. No obvious parallels offer themselves for the vegetating mood of the *tempo giusto*, the slow-movement battle zone of the *adagio* or the phased collapse of the *allegro*. The new F minor fugato is the nearest thing to an exception. It is a *danse macabre* in the manner of such devilish genre-pieces as the 'Witches' Sabbath' finale of Berlioz's *Fantastic Symphony* or Dukas's *The Sorcerer's Apprentice* (see Ex. 16).

Section B1 (fig. 71–^{1}7, bb. 410–86). Dance of Death.

The perfect fourth, bearer of so much promise at the beginning of the movement, but reduced to a forlorn cipher in **A3e**, now opens a banal fugue subject. Its repetitive insistence and its C–F level recall passages of

Ex. 17 Second movement, section B1, layout of fugal entries and contour of codettas.

non-progress in the first movement (cf. fig. 7–8, fig. 17–18). The layout of fugal entries apparently mimics academic correctness, though in fact the textbook is flouted by the second violins' real rather than tonal answer, by the violas entering at the same high pitch as the first violins, maintaining the airborne quality for longer than expected, and by the fourth entry being given to bassoons in octaves rather than to cellos (Ex. 17).

The plan of this fugal exposition may be mock-academic and the subject itself banal, and that will prove to be precisely the point. However, the counter-subject and codetta material is deployed with economy and cunning. First of all there is a free extension (codetta) before the second entry (fig. 71^{8-13}), a sufficiently unorthodox procedure to draw attention to itself and encourage the ear (if only on repeated hearings!) to fasten onto its later counterparts. The first codetta circles around the tonic triad, the first counter-subject around the dominant.

The second codetta (fig. 72^{8}–4) develops the counter-subject's undulation into longer up-and-down contours, while the one-bar delay in the violin 2 entry sets up some delicious metrical cross-accentuation, to which consistent second-beat emphasis adds dizzyingly in the five bars leading into the chromatic swoon down from fig. 73. The second counter-subject continues the high level of chromaticism and develops the y motif tailpiece of the first codetta, bringing the register up so that the third codetta can be a continuous fall.

The third codetta (fig. 74^{8}–5) introduces skittering quaver motion (recall the infiltration of quavers in section A) which the third counter-subject develops in imitation, accompanied by oscillating quavers; in the third counter-subject the first violins lead a staggered ascent which will allow the fourth codetta (fig. 75^{8}–7) to be another long fall, with a five-bar echo to conclude the fugal exposition. The fourth codetta also liquidates

61

the last motif of the fugue subject and introduces a metrically displaced version of the 'skittering' crotchet-four-quavers rhythm.

Each of these incidental contrapuntal features is logically evolved; each creates variety; each will be exploited in the later climactic stages of this mad fugue. This banal-surfaced music conceals an acrobatic cleverness which should not be under-estimated.

Section B1a (fig. 77–8, bb. 487–97). Devilish glee.

All the while the strings have been muted (since section **A3e**) and the dynamic level has been a consistent *piano* until the *diminuendo* at the very end of the fugal exposition (the violas' *mezzo piano* and bassoons' *mezzo forte* merely maintain balance with the prevailing *piano*). Our ears have been fascinated by this quietness and the intriguingly subtle processes of the contrapuntal material. The quieter the music goes the more it brings us right up close to observe it. When we are nose to nose, the mask is ripped off to reveal the authentic grimace of evil, emulating the Pan-ic cries from Nielsen's tone-poem *Pan and Syrinx* FS87, composed 1917–18. Clarinet skirls were one of the most notorious accomplices of evil in the first movement. Now they gleefully shriek out the continuous quavers that have so undermined the second movement, using the familiar distortion of the **A2** motif, the 'skittering' rhythm from the fugal exposition, and the descending scale from **A1** and **A1a** (fig. 40^{3-5}, $^{2}42$–42). Harmonically the skirls outline a neapolitan cadence (of crucial significance for the later stages of the fugue), all underpinned by an implacable dominant pedal in the timpani – cf. the first movement *adagio* crisis at fig. 34.

Section B2 (fig. 78–87, bb. 497–606). Mayhem.

All hell breaks loose. The quiet, clever exposition of **B1** was a false front. This is the real thing, the nightmare become reality. The clarinet skirls are superimposed on the first three entries of a second fugal exposition. By the end of the third entry (fig. 83) the skirls have so infected the codetta and counter-subject material that their destructiveness is implanted in the heart of the fugal texture itself. The fourth entry (fig. 83) and the first 'middle entry' (fig. 84^{8}) proceed by intensification of

Ex. 18 Second movement, section B2, fugal entries and codettas

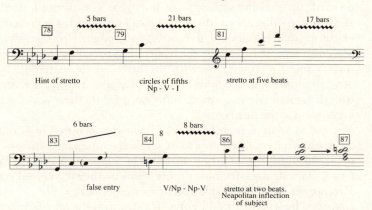

scoring; the final entry of the section (fig. 86) intensifies by means of a stretto at the fourth and at two beats' distance, with intervallic distortion of the subject to take on the neapolitan characteristics of the clarinet skirls themselves (Ex. 18).

Beyond these essential characteristics the accumulation of intensity can be followed in more detail:

1   Fig. 78. The first entry and codetta are accompanied by a hint of the stretti to come and then by clarinet skirls constructed as before from scale segments and the skittering quavers rhythm.

2   Fig. 79. The second entry is accompanied by variants on the chromatic y motif from the tailpiece of the preceding codetta. The second codetta is much extended – harmonically by two large circle-of-fifths progressions, motivically by the first signs of the clarinet scales infiltrating counter-subject material.

3   Fig. 81. The third entry is a stretto at five beats' distance, taking up the hint at the beginning of the first entry. The counter-subject material consists of up-and-down scales in the bass (perhaps a parody of the triumphant climax of the first movement – fig. 37^5–8) and of skirls now taken into the heart of the texture. The codetta (from fig. 81^8) is harmonically static on repeated half closes in C minor (contrast the extreme mobility of the previous codetta), while the stretto of the skittering quavers motif produces a turbulent rush of quavers now fully infected by the skirls.

4   Fig. 83. The fourth entry (starting on trumpets and trombones) is a

continuous intensification, expressed partly in the codetta from fig. 84 made up of rising sequences of the fugue's head-motif, partly in the counter-subject's stretto of prime and retrograde versions of the skittering quavers motif. This motif is now reduced to a skirl-derived scale segment, shadowed by the horns (thus revealing the skittering-quaver motif's connection with the first codetta material). All is strictly confined to the notes of the C melodic minor scale, and an overall rising scale is formed, influenced by the bass scales which accompanied the third entry.

5   Fig. 84[8]. The first 'middle entry' is strongly anchored to G minor. The skittering motif returns to its original contour, and the piccolo, oboe and third trumpet try to dislodge G minor with a strong $B_\natural$–G figure. Two strong harmonic progressions do the job, re-confirming F minor via an unmistakable lean to the neapolitan.

6   Fig. 86. The second 'middle entry' is a stretto at the fourth, based on an aggregate reminiscent of section **A** (see Ex. 7). Its neapolitan alteration of the second degree now seems an almost inevitable consequence of the stream of thought. The skirling quavers coalesce on written-out trills for the entire string section, recalling the 'evil' motif of the first movement. Their evolution of new shapes is subtle but significant. The F minor foundation is rock-solid, despite harmonic ructions above which tilt the ending to an added sixth, once again suggestive of the previous movement (fig. 9–10).[16]

Section B2a (fig. 87–[1]8, bb. 606–18). Frozen panic.

The accumulation of intensity in the second exposition has been remorseless. Now the needle has moved into the red and the mechanism is over-heating. The forces of evil are edging to the borderline between fury and fit. Nielsen was no stranger to that area himself – he once described himself as being so enraged he could grab hell-fire and throw it at the object of his anger;[17] the Second Symphony's Choleric Temperament and the Clarinet Concerto show how much he relished the opportunity to embody extreme rage in music, without necessarily equating it with evil.

Over a tonic F minor pedal the clarinet skirls take over the written-out-trill pattern suggested by strings and piccolo at the end of **B2** and ultimately traceable to the first movement's 'evil' motif. They are joined and affected by triplet flashes in flutes and piccolo. The quaver-to-triplet escalation witnessed in section **A** is recurring at the faster *presto* tempo. Meanwhile the outline harmony moves again to the dominant.

Section B2b (fig. 88–92, bb. 618–79). Desperation.

The evil of the fugue breaks apart by its own inability to operate within limits. The subject heaves around looking for territory to occupy, all the while contained by the written-out trill on G and $F_\sharp$, before exploding over two approach chords in F minor. The machine flies off the rails, some of its wheels still spinning (in the shape of the y motif in the flute). The flute line comes to rest on a low B. In the meantime it has effaced the triple metre and brought to rest not only the y motif and the screaming-pitch dynamics but also the fast tempo.

The frustration of this 'mad' fugue can be seen in the deepest structural level of the harmony (see Ex. 31), which, like the first movement's *adagio*, repeatedly moves to half-closes but, unlike it, is denied an affirmative resolution. Even the succeeding 'sane' fugue rests initially on the dominant C rather the tonic F.

Section C (fig. 92–¹9, bb. 679–730). Reconstruction; the 'sane' fugue.

The mad machine has self-destructed and must not be allowed to re-assemble itself. The territory it inhabited must be acknowledged and re-populated; lessons must be learnt from the mistakes which allowed it to usurp power in the first place. Nielsen expresses such processes in terms of the checks and balances of inherited musical forms, and it is time to consider once again the overall balance of his symphonic structure.

The first movement fell into two halves, the *tempo giusto* deliberately falling short of 'first movement' sonata density, harmonic momentum and pace, the *adagio* being dependent on it and deliberately falling short of slow movement structural contrast and extension. The second movement is framed as a finale whose sonata construction, harmonic complexity and pace will make good the 'deficiencies' of the first movement. Its acknowledgement of the layout of the traditional symphony include the scherzo substitute movement just heard (the 'mad' fugue). But at which point in the structure? Veijo Murtomäki, following Christopher Ballantine, feels that the *allegro* breaks off after its development section to incorporate scherzo and slow movements before the recapitulation.[18] This would suggest the kind of four-in-one structure inaugurated by Schubert's 'Wanderer' Fantasy and furthered by Liszt and Schoenberg. Fair enough. But the influence of Nielsen's psychological programme has to be borne in mind. If section **A3** was indeed a development section it was a very negative one, designed as a metaphor for collapse.[19] What the rest of the piece therefore needs, after the scherzo–equivalent 'mad' fugue, is not only a slow section to make good the deficiency of the first movement *adagio*, but also a *positive development* of the main finale material. This is precisely what Section **C** sets out to supply.

269 bars have just passed in four minutes. The next 61 will require four and a half minutes and a good deal more concentrated thought. The *andante un poco tranquillo* is another fugue, again led off by the first violins and working down through the muted string section, but this time thoughtfully transforming the **A1** theme. It will propose sanity as an antidote to madness. After the fugal exposition (**C1**) and a pastoral stretto in three flutes (**C1a**), the **A2** theme is similarly transformed in a high string passage of Sibelian sustained intensity, which turns into a retransition to the final *allegro* (**C2**).

Section C1 (fig. 92–6, bb. 679–712). Sanity.

Now that the storm has blown over it is time for reconstruction. Or maybe it is not quite time. This is the third opportunity for rebuilding and it needs to learn lessons from the past. The first lesson is patience and acceptance. For the time being the surviving personality is under no obligation to do anything, to go anywhere or to solve anything. Its immediate priority is to breathe freely and recapture a sense of the possibility of pure being, free from oppression. In the meantime self-knowledge would be a worthwhile project. So a calm dwelling on the key of F, the region associated with anything but calmness, and a reconsideration of the main theme of the opening *allegro*, are psychologically appropriate.[20]

Very well, F minor it shall be, in key signature if nothing else (curious that the main theme of the movement always carries an unexpected key signature). On its fifth entry the 'sane' fugue will still be in F, having

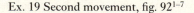

Ex. 19 Second movement, fig. 92[1-7]

strayed no further, so far as the eye is concerned, than its relative major and the dominant thereof. That straying is in itself not negligible – entries in A♭ and E♭ may be within the accepted orbit of the Bachian fugue, assuming an F minor tonic, but there they are confined to later stages than the fugal exposition. In fact the ear tells us that the mode is really F *major*, in whose terms A♭ and E♭ are only modally related cousins. So this fugue is neither academically constrained nor under pressure from latent genre-associations (compare the 'mad' fugue). It is free to think, to let its musical processes expand and interact away from the arena of ethical battles (though in the broader context it is precisely this fact which defines its ethical role).

The fugue's important condition for accepting the arena of F is that the metre and tempo have finally changed to a thoughtful common time. The nature of the fugue subject demands close consideration (Ex. 19). The tritone transposition of Theme A is exact until the last crotchet beat of the third bar, with the lower strings again supplying the **z** motif in the original place. There is now a distinction proposed, however, between the first two phrases (F major, marked *semplice*) and the third (F Dorian and marked *espress.[ivo]*). From that point there is, as in the 'mad' fugue, free codetta material.

Ex. 20 Second movement, section C1 entries and codettas

One fundamental difference from the 'mad' fugue is that the entries are not bound to a quasi-academic reinforcement of the tonic. Indeed the opening of the fugue never sits down on a root position tonic at all, but rests on a six-four dominant. The following entries shift to the 'relative' major (A♭) and its dominant before completing a five-voice exposition with entries in the home dominant and tonic. The codetta material will shadow this process by adding upward-striving contours to the two 'foreign' key entries and arc-shaped ones to the rest. This in turn determines the initial contour of the counter-subjects (Ex. 20).

Within this context the 'free breathing' of the fugue can be examined in a little more detail.

1   In the first codetta (fig. 92[5–7]) the major–minor ambivalence of the theme is retained, after which the three chromatic degrees of the scale not present in the subject are introduced in turn. The raised tonic forms part of a diminished third figure, and the flat sixth is poetically dwelt on in a clash with the dominant (see Ex. 19). Both chromatic degrees will be highlighted features in the rest of the exposition. The fact that Nielsen has been operating so consistently with diatonic modes in the first movement (however complex their interaction) and with arcs on the circle of fifths in the second, means that such chromaticisms (as indeed the strained intervals of the collapse phases of the *allegro*) register with a telling strangeness.

2   The E♮ at the end of the first codetta pivots as the flat sixth of the second entry – in A♭ (fig. 92[7]). For the first two bars of the counter-subject the pivot function remains, as the first violin line gently holds on to its prior F tonality. These two bars, against the *semplice* element of the subject, establish a gentle scalewise motion, harmonically floating, which is again part of the template for the fugue, without ever becoming a regular counter-subject. The flat sixth is again dwelt on against the dominant, the raised tonic again partakes in a beautiful diminished third figure, and a flattened fifth now features more prominently. All three added chromaticisms form poignant disso-

nances with the *espressivo* element of the subject material, while the second codetta very briefly echoes the turning figure of the first and ascends in an exquisite *diminuendo*.

3   In the third entry (fig. 93–4) the floating scalewise counterpoint to the *semplice* element (now no longer marked as such, perhaps because the violas are expected to have got the message) is retained. Once again it carries over the previous tonality (A♭) rather than immediately confirming that of the subject entry (E♭). Once again the missing three chromatic degrees are introduced in rapid succession against the *espressivo* element, but with the intensity supplied more by the concentrated interweaving of angular lines than by vertical dissonance. In response to the condensing in the second entry, both the *espressivo* and codetta fields are now expanded. The third codetta celebrates the chromaticism and upward striving of the second, climbing from the dominant to the tonic of E♭ and on through C to A minor, at which point the delayed diminished third leads into the dominant of the next C entry.

4   Above the fourth entry (fig. 94–5) the counterpoint falls scalewise as before. It is now calmer above the *espressivo* element, before erupting via a diminished third to the neapolitan (the three 'missing' chromatic degrees thus appear in quick succession). The strongest dominant preparation in the fugue sets up the final entry in F.

5   High tessitura string writing has lent a special intensity to the fugue so far. Indeed the entire exposition to this point can be comfortably notated in the treble clef. The final entry sits down with solid horn and bassoon timbre, but an almost continuous inverted dominant pedal nevertheless keeps the music airborne. Like all the previous entries this one features calm stepwise motion in the counterpoint, followed by yearning chromaticisms (but no D♭s – the one in the first violins, fig. 95[1], is a misprint in the 1950 score), and an expressive dynamic swelling in the codetta. At the last moment F minor is turned into an approach to an imperfect cadence in C.

Section C1a (fig. 96–[1]7, bb. 712–16). Relaxing.

Has the 'sane' fugue achieved nothing more than an imperfect cadence? It may not have anything to show in terms of new ground won, but it has at least established that self-possession and freedom of thought are possible. The return to F is no admission of failure; rather it is a sign of acceptance and confidence that there is nothing to fear. The transfiguration of F has been poetry in motion. Three flutes now embark on a pastoral-sounding stretto, paraphrasing the second phrase of the fugue subject in a very clear C major, incorporating the Nielsenesque mixolydian seventh. Quite unobtrusively the fourths of the theme have given way to thirds and arpeggiations of a tonic triad.

The five bars of **C1a** are remarkably passive. By design. The 'sane' fugue has therapeutically rediscovered freedom of movement and feeling, and the flutes' pendant to it can now bask in a regained arcadia. There are three structural-dramatic issues here. First, this is a way of discovering that non-thematic or liquidating passages, previously the bane of the symphony, are nothing to fear; second, the liquidation of the perfect fourth (see flute 3) quietly re-introduces a 'periheletic' figure[21] which mollifies the wild version of it heard in the clarinets during the 'mad' fugue (see fig. 87^{1-5}) and which will play a role in the final stages of the work (see section **D2c** below) in exorcising the written-out trill of the 'evil' motif; third, and most important, the unemphatic but securely established C major is a sharpwards rise from F, which is the antidote to the fatal flatwards falls that so undermined the **A** section.

Section C2 (fig. ^{1}97–^{1}9, bb. 716–30). Psyching up.

The **A1** theme has now been given the positive development it was denied in the pseudo-development of **A3a–e**. Now it is the **A2** theme's turn for transformation. It is at the same pitch as its original appearance, but in timbre, tempo, metre and tonality it is reinterpreted. The high string texture lends it the same passionate intensity as the preceding fugal exposition, reinforced by the slow tempo and quadruple metre, while the counter-melody in the high cellos emphasises the element of thoughtful reconstruction. Above all, the tonal orientation is in the region of G, with sharp-side harmonies to the fore. In other words, this is another sharpwards move (from the F of section **C1** through the C of **C1a**) with the strong implied potential to move further in the same direction.

The original end of the **A2** theme (see Ex. 11) is paraphrased, allowing for some free contrapuntal fantasising, including a falling line which contains a strong Nielsen fingerprint – self-assertion continues. The restatement of the theme, still at original pitch, continues the sharp-wards rise. It is over a D pedal with tendencies to pull sharpwards to A and E (and to sustain the notes of the theme itself). No fewer than six contrapuntal voices are now active, over-trumping the five-voiced fugal exposition of **C1**.

Not only is the original tailpiece now intact, the answering phrase is also at original pitch. Once again D is the focus, but the pull to E is adjusted towards a C$_\sharp$ bass with falling inner parts. The harmony is familiar (see fig. 56⁷–7), but instead of being at a forlorn distance from the 'home' B, as in the prolonged liquidation of **A3b**, it now pulls strongly in that very same direction.

The strategy of the entire **C** section is now clear. The new thoughtful-ness goes hand in hand with a quietly purposeful sharpwards orienta-tion, again using D as a staging-post, but this time in a positive direction (see Ex. 32). Each stage of this sharpwards movement is more problem-atic than the previous one. The move from F to C follows naturally from the subject-answer paradigm of the fugal exposition and is given approach-dominant preparation; the move from C to G has repeated cadential confirmation but not preparation; the move to D is neither pre-pared nor confirmed in an orthodox functional way, but rather is pro-posed by a centre of gravity pulling the harmony to an arc on the circle of fifths and extending past it towards A and E.

No doubt a straightforward reversal of the flatwards drift of Section **A** (itself a far from straightforward affair) would have been crassly simplis-tic. It is enough at this stage that a declaration of intent has been issued, on the basis of a new self-determination and will-power.[22]

Section D (fig. 99–114¹⁵, bb. 731–903)

The final section of the piece is less than half the length of section **A**, whose material it recapitulates and recasts. That is no surprise if section **A** is considered an exposition and development combined. But the reca-pitulatory element of section **D** covers only 67 bars (fig. 99–105) corre-sponding to **A**'s 150 of exposition (opening–fig. 51⁸), while a 106-bar coda (fig. 105–end) recapitulates the 'quasi-development' (the 260 bars of **A3a–e**). Whichever way we look at it the final section is a remarkably concentrated affair.

This can simply be viewed in a critical light. Voices have been raised to the effect that the conclusion is not entirely satisfactory, and it is well known that Nielsen was composing in a furious hurry to meet his deadline for performance (not for the first time in his life). On the other hand, for anyone engaged on a major creative project it is not unusual that once the last psychological hurdles have been crossed the final stages may come in a rush of rapid hard work. In this instance the major hurdle has been overcome in the thoughtful recasting of themes A1 and A2 in the 'sane' fugue; indeed it could be said that this recasting is an integral part of the whole process of recapitulation, even though it apparently stands outside the formal borderlines. Given that psychological growth and absorption is Nielsen's aim, rather than heaven-storming apotheosis, this may be enough to safeguard the proportions of the music. It may still not be enough to make the sense of structural inevitability guaranteed, and it would be quite a challenge to argue that Nielsen's E♭ conclusion measures up to those of Sibelius's Fifth, or Mahler's Second or Eighth, even allowing for the obvious difference in expressive aims. To my mind the blame for any serious feeling of let-down, if such there be, should be laid squarely at the door of conductors rather than the composer. There is a special type of ecstasy behind the notes, and it does not take a huge effort of imagination or intellect to tap into it or to communicate it in performance.

The broad relationship of material in sections **A** and **D** may be tabulated as follows (Ex. 21).

Section D1 (fig. 99–100³, bb. 731–51). Reassertion; drift.

The recapitulation of theme **A** is re-scored for a *fortissimo* balance with significantly more emphasis on the theme itself (including the brightness of higher octave doubling at the beginning and end) and less on the flatwards-pulling E trill. The two bars of repeated E^7 chords (fig. 40$^{1–3}$) at the end of the section are elided; there is a sense of urgency, impatience even, of needing to confront past issues with new vigour.

Section D1a (fig. 100³–¹2, bb. 751–63). Strong jolt.

Thus far, and no further. Down to a comfortable A major is as far as Nielsen allows his recapitulation to slip. Instead of resisting with quasi-

Ex. 21 Second movement, sections A and D, comparison

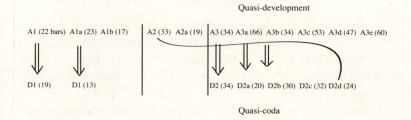

bitonality and short-circuiting from the next fall to D (see section **A1a**), he immediately throws a spanner in the works and diverts to the sharp side of B. Is the strings' scale representative of F, B♭, E♭, A♭ or D♭/C♯ (compare the scale at fig. ²40)? A case could be made for any of these, or for a progression from one to the other, or, perhaps most realistically, for an orientation somewhere on that arc of the circle of fifths, preparing for a clarification of a narrower arc centred on C♯ and F♯. The quavers at fig. ²102 are in a doubled-back shape, not previously used, which seems determined to reinforce the dominant of B. Again all elements of repetition or vacillation have been purged, and the sub-section is cut short.

Section D2 (fig. 102–5, bb. 764–98).
Exhilaration; warning.

The journey towards the conclusion is still a rough ride. The engine may be more trustworthy now, but it is untested on a still uncertain and previously hazardous surface. Section **D2** is a minor third downward transposition of **A3**, with subtle reinforcements and brightenings in the scoring. Its harmonic direction involves the major-third axis transposed to E–C–A♭; and the final digression is turned towards C minor. The final gesture of the section is, crucially, a *crescendo* instead of a *diminuendo* (fig. ¹105, cf. fig. 51[8]), another sign that the depressing collapse of section **A3** is going to be resisted and turned around.

Section D2a (fig. 105–[1]7, bb. 798–817). Turbulent searching. Absorbing.

Now more aggressive, though still dynamically repressed, the unison string quavers continue the minor third downward transposition for a further 50 bars (fig. 105–10 = fig. [4]52–[1]56); fig. 107[3–7] is slightly adjusted from fig. 53[2–9] in order to fit with a compressed version of Theme **A2**.

The section starts from G as dominant of C minor, and the trumpets' and horns' repeated Ds emphasise G's own dominant. A climb back sharpwards to the 'home' tonic of B is of course an option, but these repeated Ds are far too reminiscent of the pre-'mad'-fugue limbo area of **A3e** for comfort. Still, the attempt to abridge and recast the collapse of **A3a–e** is bold (and it is emboldened by the similar abridgment of Section **D1**). The horns and trumpets raise the stakes and propose repeated Fs; the harmonic indifference of the unison strings is no obstacle – in late-romantic harmony anything can be brought within the ambit of a domi-nant pedal. The next step matches the minor third ascent from D to F and 'raises' it to a perfect fourth – to B♭. So begins the 70-bar dominant pedal which will eventually confirm E♭ as the goal tonality of the sym-phony. Terrific momentum is generated by the transformation of the crotchet repeated notes into whooping octaves in the horns and trum-pets,[23] an early sign of former negatives being changed to positives. The second hornist has the privilege of knowing that the idea for this was dis-creetly planted in the *adagio* theme of the first movement (cf. fig. 26[2–3]).

Section D2b (fig. 107–[1]10, bb. 817–47). Acclaiming.

The entire woodwind choir chant Theme **A2**. The *fortissimo* unison is an antidote to the rushing strings far stronger than the four-octave spacing of flute and bassoon at the corresponding place in **A3a** (see fig. 53–4). The harmonic relationship between theme and accompaniment has changed. In **A3a** they were temporarily united in re-proposing B major; here they form an intensified version of the movement's fundamental harmonic aggregate (see Exx. 7, 11), and this would seem to be a prime reason behind the entire minor third transposition of **D2**.

The shifting pedal-points of the horns and trumpets in **D2a** were like the searchings of a chess computer for the best move. Given an infinite amount of time the best move will be found. Music, however, at least Western symphonic music, derives its power from temporal limitations, and within Nielsen's limitations the discovery of the dominant of E♭ will prove a revelation (see below, section **D2c**).

The harmonised version of theme **A2** is played in irregular descending sequence, now returned to an exact lower-minor-third transposition of the first wave of such progressions in **A3a** (fig. 108–10, cf. fig. 54–^{2}56). This gives the dominant pedal plenty still to chew on before it can resolve. All the while an expanding phrase-structure has broadened the lung-capacity of the music (from fig. 105^2, the entry of the horns and trumpets, the phrase-structure is 5+6+8+11+11+8 bars).

Section D2c (fig. 110–^{1}13, bb. 848–79). Engulfing.

On pp. 54 and 61 of his draft score, under the beginning of **D1** and the end of **D2** respectively (cf. figs. 97–9 and 104) Nielsen sketched ideas for the final section of the movement. Clearly the idea of E♭ as a goal tonality had presented itself to him, even if his draft offers no clue as to any rationale that may have involved.

On his arrival at the opening of **D2c** Nielsen wrote above the stave 'Es dur fortegn' [E♭ major key signature]. This crucial point in the composition marks the turn away from the material of section **A** and the beginning of the home stretch. The excitement of the dominant pedal derives from two main things: first, that it is sustained long enough to swallow up all the tide of dissonance that has previously depressed the music; second, that it witnesses the transformation of formerly negative themes into positives. The pedal is in itself one such transformation; the inert repeated notes which blighted **A3e** have been re-energised into yodelling, hemiola-defined octave leaps.

The process continues, intensified in urgency by the addition of timpani to the dominant pedal. The string quavers break off and fall into a dispute – the woodwind have the oscillating trill shape heard at the highpoint of the 'mad' fugue (see fig. 86–7, 88–90) and derived ultimately from the first movement's 'evil' motif, but with a new chromatic upbeat; the strings have the same rhythm, but the shape derives from the clarinet episodes of the 'mad' fugue (see fig. 87$^{1-5}$) by way of the pastoral episode of the 'sane' fugue (fig. 96–7). The clarinets' nihilism is being contained, as before, by the dominant pedal, and swept along and engulfed, as never before, by the rhythmic pulsation.

The opposition between wind and strings recalls the battle-zone of the first movement, as does the containing pedal-point (cf. fig. 33–7). Meanwhile the rising sequences carefully avoid the pedal B♭, but throw every other note of the chromatic scale against it. A second phase begins at fig. ^{4}112 and ascends in chromatic doubled thirds to B♭, *in alt*, at which point the suppressed phase of theme **A2** from section **A3a** returns (fig. 112–13, cf. fig. 56$^{1-8}$, allowing for the same minor third downward transposition, see Ex. 21). Also engulfed here are the tritones applied to the end of Theme **B**. Meanwhile the strings are nagging furiously at the tonic E♭, before ascending in a magnificent scale to their high B♭s (a gesture echoed, probably unwittingly, by Shostakovich in the coda to his Fifth Symphony). The entire arc-shaped construction of **D2c** recalls the framing of **A3c**.

Section D2d (fig. 113–14^{15}, bb. 880–903). Exaltation.

The life-force is surging; the New Man is born; the music is free to surf to its conclusion. At last there is a notated slowing. Section A's gradual loss of control was emphasised by increases in tempo. Now the slowing, combined with dynamic intensification, confirms exaltation in the achievement of control. The pulsating B♭ crotchets are held aloft, gradually giving way to a tonic pedal which makes consonant the aggravating trill from the beginning of the movement. The crotchets then transfer to the timpani, completing the apotheosis of the repeated note which defies and reverses the vegetating of the first movement and the collapse from activity into vegetating in the second.[24] Theme **A2** is proclaimed in a triumphant revolving brass canon, while the quasi-trill is heard yet again on the flat seventh, as it was originally in the 'evil' motif. Finally the horn-call itself (cf. **A3c**) is combined with the flat seventh, as never before in the symphony. With that, virtually every force previously associated with a negative psychic disposition has contributed to a triumph which is truly earned. The only anomaly left at the end is the bassoon's inaudible insistence on trilling on the dominant – perhaps a last remnant of the fourths-based sonority of the movement?[25]

Like the conclusion of Sibelius's Fifth, this is no easily manufactured apotheosis. Unlike it, the key of E♭ is pulled out of the hat rather than regained. Hints of E♭ have admittedly been present throughout the symphony.[26] And apart from this fact its fitness can be justified in various ways, some of them more ingenious than convincing – as a major third ascent from B, echoing the 'positive' move from G to B in the first movement's *adagio*; as a flat seventh to the fatal F, undermining it just as A undermined B in the second movement; as the tritonal antagonist to the same A.[27] If that dramatic view of tonality is accepted in principle (a fairly major 'if') it will indeed be found that no other key so satisfyingly fits the bill. But I would be inclined to place equal emphasis on two broader points – the freshness of a key untainted with negative associations elsewhere in the work; and the association of E♭ with life-asserting symphonic endings, from Beethoven's 'Eroica' through Mahler's Second and Eighth to Sibelius' Fifth. What is just as important as the theoretical justification is Nielsen's inner conviction. However well- or ill-founded theoretically, it is this conviction which enables him to make the explicit thematic associations he does with the confidence that they are founded on the bedrock of a convincing tonal scheme. It is the thematic associations which do the active work, the tonality that supplies the foundation – whether for the listener or only for the composer is secondary.[28]

These then are the enabling forces for one of the great endings in the symphonic literature. It may not spell out its message in capital letters, and its power comes as much from its self-containment as from any beside-itself ecstasy. But the distance travelled from the slough of despond of the *allegro* and the near-insanity of the *presto* is immense. And the control with which the recovery is managed in the *andante* is as impressive as the control with which the collapse was conveyed. To express these things with such precision and within the perspectives of a post-classical musical language is an achievement for which greatness does not seem a hyperbolic description.

Reviewing Godtfred Skjerne's *Plutarks dialog om musiken*, Nielsen wrote in the *Orkesterforeningens medlemsblad* of November 1909, 'Our work is... a continual protest against the thought of death and an appeal to and cry for life.'[29] That certainly seems to be the arena in which the Fifth

Symphony has been playing out its drama. The strength of its protest is matched by the urgency of its appeal, and Nielsen does not wait passively for any outside force to give answer. He seeks it with all the willpower of a man in his physical prime and with all the craftsmanship of a symphonist at the peak of his powers. The result is one of music's greatest revenges on the pain of life.

4

Composition, reception, editions, recordings

Composition

After his resignation as conductor of the Royal Opera in 1914, and until the time of the Fifth Symphony, Nielsen's professional life consisted mainly of conducting the Copenhagen *Musikforening*[1] and guest appearances with Stenhammar's *Orkesterförening* in Gothenburg. When in Denmark he generally stayed either with his son-in-law Eggert Møller in Copenhagen's Nørrebrogade or in the summer villa 'Højbo' in Humlebæk, the property of his businessman-friend and former pupil Carl Johan Michaelsen.[2] It was not until January 1922, just after completion of the symphony that his differences with his wife were resolved to the extent that they could live together again in their State-owned artists' house in Frederiksholms Kanal No. 28a.

There is no surviving documentation of the beginning of Nielsen's work on the Fifth Symphony or of his initial motivation. The first movement was composed in Humlebæk during the winter and spring of 1921. On 17 February Nielsen reported to Telmányi that he had made passable but slow progress,[3] yet on 4 March he told his wife that the first movement was finished. A further letter to Telmányi on 23 March again told of slow progress, and on the 31st of that month he announced to his wife that he had made a fair copy of the first movement but had come to a stop with the rest of the composition and was afraid that his creative gifts were deserting him; he would take the 'usual remedy' of turning to J. S. Bach for inspiration.[4] At the beginning of the summer he spent some time at the summer house he had bought three years earlier at Skagen; at the end of July and August he stayed at Damgaard, the Jutland home of his friend Charlotte Trap de Thygeson, where he had to break off work on the symphony to compose the cantata *Springtime on Fyn*, fulfilling a promise to the Danish Choral Society.[5] Later that autumn he went as usual to Gothenburg to conduct for a few months, using every free moment to work on the second movement, often from 10 o'clock in the morning until 5 o'clock the next morning, although he still had a way to go when he wrote to Mrs Vera Michaelsen on 9 December that it was the most difficult task he had yet given himself.[6]

Nielsen completed the symphony on 15 January 1922, nine days before conducting its first performance at the *Musikforening* together with Beethoven's Leonora Overture No. 2, Bach's First Brandenburg Concerto and the cantata 'Christ lag in Todesbanden'.[7] One memory of this performance was that the orchestra had had insufficient rehearsal time and were struggling to cope with error-ridden parts for the new work; nevertheless Nielsen's conducting managed to put his concept across.[8]

Reception

The first movement was especially well received in the following day's press. Several reviewers noted similarities with *Aladdin* and Nielsen's other theatrical or programmatic scores.[9] Axel Kjerulf, perhaps with inside information from the composer, wrote in *Politiken* of the exotic, pastoral dreamworld in the *tempo giusto* giving way to an Arabian march. In the *Adagio* Kjerulf heard a Dream giving way to a 'Dream about Deeds... Carl Nielsen has maybe never written more powerful, beautiful, fundamentally healthy [*kærnesund*] and genuine music than here'; but he found the second movement more puzzling: 'remarkable music, brilliantly made – but what does it have to say to us?' His conclusion was 'more Dream than Deeds' [*mere Drøm end Daad*].[10] Musicians' opinions were divided. A surprising rejection came from a long-time supporter and friend, Victor Bendix, who wrote to Nielsen the day after the première, calling the work a 'Sinfonie filmatique, this dirty trenches-music, this impudent fraud, this clenched fist in the face of a defenceless, novelty-snobbish, titillation-sick public, commonplace people *en masse*, who lovingly lick the hand stained with their own noses' blood!'[11]

Nielsen repeated the symphony at Gothenburg's *Orkesterförening* on 8 March, mentioning to his wife that he needed more rehearsals to cope with the extreme difficulties of the second movement.[12] He conducted the German première in Berlin on 1 December 1922, in a concert of his own music including the 'Maskarade' Overture, the Violin Concerto and the piano Chaconne. The press was divided. A positive reception came from Max Seiffert in *Die Musik*, a negative one from the anonymous critic of the *Deutsche Allgemeine Zeitung* who suspected that the visit was founded on the advantageous exchange rate with the Danish currency, and who reckoned that Germany had enough bad composers without importing them; he found nothing in the series of Nielsen concerts that had not been said by Wagner, Liszt and Brahms fifty years earlier. Oscar Bie in the *Berliner Börsen Courier* observed that 'The Fifth Symphony, in two movements, with its Nature scenes and string chorale was reminiscent of Mahler's technique, but not so primordially felt: a not quite coherent assembly of desired vision and skilful art.'[13]

The Swedish performance on 20 January 1924, conducted by Georg Schneevoigt, caused a famous scandal.[14] The *Berlingske Tidende* reported that a section of the public could not take the modernism of the work:

> Midway through the first part with its rattling drums and 'cacophonous' effects a genuine panic broke out. Around a quarter of the audience rushed for the exits with confusion and anger written over their faces, and those who remained tried to hiss down the 'spectacle', while the conductor Georg Schneevoigt drove the orchestra to extremes of volume. This whole intermezzo underlined the humoristic-burlesque element in the symphony in such a way that Carl Nielsen could certainly never have dreamed of. His representation of modern life with its confusion, brutality and struggle, all the uncontrolled shouts of pain and ignorance – and behind it all the side drum's harsh rhythm as the only disciplining force – as the public fled, made a touch of almost diabolic humour.[15]

Nevertheless the Swedes soon took to the symphony, as reviews of the Stockholm concert on 5 December 1928 make clear – see chapter 2, note 30.

Nielsen also conducted the Fifth Symphony in Oslo on 4 November 1926,[16] and it was well received in Paris at the Salle Gaveau on 21 October 1926 under Nielsen's son-in-law Emil Telmányi in part of a concert including the then new Flute Concerto. It was on this occasion that Honegger made the declaration already quoted (see above, p. 10).

Among Nielsen's guiding principles as a conductor were to let everything devolve from a correct tempo and not to disturb fine musicians when they were playing well.[17] When he heard others interpreting his own work he sometimes found those principles coming into conflict. On 1 July 1927 Wilhelm Furtwängler conducted the Fifth Symphony for the festival of the International Society for Contemporary Music in Frankfurt, Rudolph Simonsen having succeeded in persuading a committee meeting in London to accept it.[18] He repeated the work at a Gewandhaus concert in Leipzig on 27 October. After the second Frankfurt rehearsal Nielsen told his wife that all was going well.[19] He later reported in *Politiken* that he might have wished some things at the beginning of the first movement otherwise, but that he preferred to let the conductor follow his convictions, particularly as he had witnessed Bartók's constant irritating interventions during rehearsals for the latter's First Piano Concerto. Overall he was somewhat disappointed that the symphony did not have more success or make an international breakthrough as a result of this occasion.[20] To Telmányi he was more specific. He was disappointed with the tameness of the 'inoffensive' side drummer, and with Furtwängler's slow tempo for the *adagio*; but following his own principle of granting fine performers licence he took the attitude, 'just let him' [*lad ham bare*]. Nevertheless for the Leipzig performance Furtwängler corrected his tempi.[21] The excessively slow tempi are confirmed by Nielsen's pupil Finn Høffding, who also mentions that the public's enthusiasm was not reflected in the lukewarm reviews.[22] On the other hand Ludvig Dolleris reports that hearing Furtwängler ask for the clarinet to be more 'hysterical' was the kind of initiative that gladdened Nielsen's heart.[23] A photograph of Furtwängler rehearsing the symphony may be found in Johannes Fabricius's pictorial biography.[24]

On 15 November 1927 the Concertgebouw performed the Fifth Symphony under Pierre Monteux, and Nielsen was amazed by the orchestra's handling of the second movement.[25] However, his daughter reports that he did not approve of the Frenchman's interpretation in general, and her husband, Telmányi, ascribed this to Monteux's being too 'neat and precise'.[26] Nielsen himself conducted the work again in Stockholm at the *Koncertförening* on 5 December 1928. After his death in 1931, the performance history of the work can be followed through the many commercial recordings.

In 1932 Hermann D. Koppel included the Fifth Symphony in a short-list of the most important Nielsen works for the generation of Danish composers which followed him (along with the first movement of the 'Espansiva', *Aladdin*, both operas, the clarinet concerto and the piano works).[27] There is no doubt that respectable symphonists such as Jørgen Bentzon and Vagn Holmboe were strongly influenced.[28] Already in the 1940s, however, the over-shadowing influence of Nielsen on the succeeding generation of Danish composers was evoking resistance from such neo-classically orientated composers as Knudåge Riisager.[29] Nearer our day Danish composers have voiced more equivocal assessment of Nielsen's influence, although most, including eventually Riisager himself, still acknowledge the force of the Fifth Symphony.[30] Nielsen's highly personal mixture of idioms and idiosyncratic approach to large-scale processes has militated against his international influence, though many of his ideals and musical images coincide with those of Shostakovich, and direct influence is traceable in the work of British symphonists such as Robert Simpson and John McCabe.

Editions

BM Borups Musikforlag, 1926, reprinted by Edwin F. Kalmus & Co., Inc. (A5659), with introduction by Clark McAllister, March 1983
SM Skandinavisk Musikforlag, 1950, ed. Emil Telmányi and Erik Tuxen
CE Complete Edition, ca. 1997, ed. Michael Fjeldsøe, Wilhelm Hansen

Nielsen failed to obtain satisfactory terms for the publication of his symphony with his usual publishers, Wilhelm Hansen Edition,[31] so he turned to his friend Carl Johan Michaelsen. Michaelsen had become a wealthy businessman but had maintained his musical interests, and in 1922 he financed the publishing firm, Hans Borups Musikforlag. The 1926 publication of the Fifth Symphony was the firm's first major project, and Nielsen received 2000 kroner for the work.[32]

In 1950 a new full score was published by Skandinavisk Musikforlag with a brief commentary and selective list of revisions by conductor Erik Tuxen (the commentary and list were omitted in the study score published at the same time). The editorial changes, which go far beyond those admitted by Tuxen, have been repeatedly criticised. Emil Telmányi, credited in the Foreword as joint-editor with Tuxen, later censured the latter for going beyond the 'necessary' retouches to the orchestration. Not that he doubted that some of Tuxen's initiatives were effective in countering reactions to the music such as Toscanini's '*Un poco troppo rumoroso*' [rather too noisy]).[33]

Both Tuxen and Telmányi were closely associated with Nielsen in his later years. Telmányi conducted the Fifth Symphony on 21 October 1926 in Paris and was entrusted by Nielsen with the care of his music should he die. Tuxen conducted the work on many occasions and three of his performances have appeared in various recordings (see below, pp. 87–8). No doubt the many changes these two made were based on their experiences conducting the work, as their editorial note claims. But there is no evidence that these changes had the composer's sanction. On the contrary, since the first score was published four years after the first performance, Nielsen had every opportunity to make changes on the basis of his own performing experience should he have felt so inclined. The only partial exception to this observation is the opening of the second movement, where the awkward melodic trumpet part seen in the first publication was not present at all in the composer's first pencil draft but was introduced by the time of the fair copy. Anyone who considers the addition ill-judged (since the problem of balance it presumably addresses is rectifiable within the rest of the texture as presented in SM) could therefore point to the evidence of Nielsen's first thoughts.

An undoubted practical improvement in SM is the increased frequency of rehearsal numbers, although even this may be said to suppress the composer's view of the structural divisions. Other changes in notation are more questionable. As mentioned in chapter 3 above, Nielsen's three-sharps key signature for the *Allegro* has been eliminated,[34] and much of the string writing in the second movement (from fig. [4]52 and from fig. 105) has been enharmonically changed, obscuring the tonal orientation of these passages. Any gains in readability seem minimal, though it has to be said that the strings in Tuxen's recordings sound far more confident using (presumably) the revised parts in 1955 than (again presumably) the original parts in 1950. Other changes in SM concern matters of scoring, articulation and dynamics.

In 1994 the commencement of a new Nielsen Complete Edition was announced, under the general editorship of Niels Martin Jensen, with the Fifth Symphony as one of its first projects, edited by Michael Fjeldsøe. This will be based on BM and will include new orchestral parts. A full critical commentary will be retained on CD ROM. In the meantime, the following summary of the most gross editorial interventions and misprints in SM may be useful. It lays no claim to comprehensiveness, but it takes into account observations from the Preface to the Edwin Kalmus reprint of the BM, by Clark McAllister, and also a private list of discrepancies compiled by British conductor Jonathan del Mar. Where significant errors in the parts are liable to be missed, or have gone uncorrected in commercial recordings, I have also listed these. As the 1950 score is in wider circulation, I shall refer to its pagination and rehearsal numbering. Unless otherwise indicated, the source corrected is the SM score, the source of correction is BM.

First movement

p.3   Orchestral parts (SM) Fig. ^{1}3, flute 2 misprinted B♭ for B♮

21   Fig. 17^7, third horn, first note should be B♭ (concert E♭)

34   Fig. $^{2-1}$22, clarinet 1 part omits tie over the bar-line

43   Fig. 25$^{6-7}$, flute part correct in both scores but given to oboe in SM parts; on last bar of page BM has no tempo marking for oboe

44   BM opening marked *adagio*

50   Fig. 30, cellos, first note should be D♯

57/8   Fig. 33^{5,8}, BM strings slurred (in crotchet beats); separate bows and accented only from fig. 34^2. This original version seems to imply an intensification in response to the re-entry of the side drum.

59   Fig. 34^2 BM side drum has instruction (in French and German): 'From [fig. 34] to [fig. ^{1}37] the side drum plays in its own tempo as if it wanted at all costs to disturb [Fr. *troubler*, Ger. *stören*] the music. The drummer controls his own beat by a metronome placed in front of him set to [crotchet=] 116'

60   Fig. 35, side drum, third–last note dotted crotchet

61/7   Fig. 35^2–^{1}37, in his Preface to the Kalmus reprint of BM

Clark McAllister claims that the trumpet parts have been substantially rewritten in SM, with transpositions and deletions. This is not the case. The only alterations, apart from accents to staccatos, are at fig. 36 and 36^3 where BM had two semiquavers for the first two notes.

64   Fig. ^{236} BM: 'The side drum now improvises with all possible fantasy, although from time to time he must pause'

67   Fig. ^{137} BM: 'At a sign from the conductor the side drum rejoins the orchestral texture.' At the last quaver BM has the side drum *molto crescendo*

74   BM instruction for repeated bar reads: 'the *diminuendo* is to be repeated until the conductor judges that the side drum sounds quite distant. The pause of the clarinets [sic] and strings should be held for a while after.'

Second movement

75–124, 150–64   Beginning to fig. 71, fig. 99–110, BM three sharps key signature

94   Strings *crescendo* at ^{551}, not at ^{751}

95   Fig. 51, BM horns, cellos and double basses as Ex. 22
           SM has assimilated these parts to fig. 104

96   Fig. $^{5–1}52$, BM cellos and basses as Ex. 23

97   BM horns notated F♯–D♯. Each horn holds the higher note for one more bar, the E♭/D♯ coming at ^{653}. Information in Kalmus reprint preface incorrect

102/5   Fig. $57–^158$, BM trombone and tuba line played by each instrument in turn, the doubling starting on the crotchet upbeat to fig. 58

108/112   Fig. 60–3, BM cello and double bass triplets not reinforced by timpani. The draft score indicates that the timpani figured in Nielsen's original scoring; therefore SM may be a justified correction

118   Fig. 66^9, violin 1, second note B♭

128   Fig. 80^{11}, bassoons, cellos and basses as Ex. 24

131   Fig. ^{282}, violin 2 second beat should be A♮

132   Fig. $82^{8–9}$, cellos and double basses as Ex. 25

Ex. 22 Second movement, fig. ¹51–51⁴, as in 1926 score

Ex. 23 Second movement, fig. ⁵⁻¹52, as in 1926 score

Ex. 24 Second movement, fig. 80¹¹, as in 1926 score

Ex. 25 Second movement, fig. 82⁸⁻⁹, as in 1926 score

136/7	Fig. 85²,⁴, horns – no *fzf* or *fzff*; fig. 85⁴⁻⁵, horns 1 and 2 crotchets should be E♭
139	Fig. 87², timpani no reduction to *mf*
147	Fig. 95, violin 1 second note should be D♮
152	Fig. 100, timpani B (cf. fig. 40)
157	Fig. 104², violin 1 main note should be A♭

Recordings

Numbers in italic indicate compact discs available at time of writing [October 1996]

1   Danish Radio Symphony Orchestra, Georg Høeberg. 2 February 1933, Copenhagen.
Danacord DACO 134–8 [1983] DACOCD 365–7 [1996]

2   Danish State Radio Symphony Orchestra, Erik Tuxen. 13, 14, 16 April 1950, Copenhagen.
HMV 2CS 2779–87, HMV Z 7022–6, EM29 04443 [1985]

3   Danish Radio Symphony Orchestra, Erik Tuxen. Edinburgh Festival 29 August 1950 (live).   Danacord DACO 121–3 [1985]

4   Danish Radio Symphony Orchestra, Thomas Jensen. 7 April 1954. Decca LXT 2980, ECS 570; Dutton Laboratories *CDLXT 2502* [1995]

5   Danish Radio Symphony Orchestra, Erik Tuxen. Paris 22 April 1955 (live).   Danacord DACOCD *351–3* [1994]

6   New York Philharmonic Orchestra, Leonard Bernstein. 1962.
CBS SBRG 72110, *SMK 47598* [1993]

7   Berlin Symphony Orchestra, Günther Herbig. 1966.
Eterna 8 20 666, Berlin Classics *0030982BC* [1995]

8   New Philharmonia Orchestra, Jascha Horenstein. 14–15 May 1969.   Unicorn(-Kanchana) RHS 300, UKCD 2023 [1989]

9   L'Orchestre de la Suisse Romande, Paul Kletzki. 1970.
Decca SXL 6491

10   New Philharmonia Orchestra, Jascha Horenstein. London, 26 February 1971.   BBC Radio Classics *15656 91492* [1996]

11   London Symphony Orchestra, Ole Schmidt. 1973–4, London. Unicorn[-Kanchana] RHS 324–30 [1974], UKCD 2000–2 [1988]

12 Bournemouth Symphony Orchestra, Paavo Berglund. 1975.
               EMI ASD 3063, EMX 2033 [1983]

13 Danish Radio Symphony Orchestra, Herbert Blomstedt. 1975.
                 EMI SLS 5027, 057 02649

14 Scottish National Orchestra, Alexander Gibson. 7 September
  1977.   RCA RL25148, *CHAN 6533* [1991]

15 Concertgebouw Orchestra, Kirill Kondrashin. 20 November 1980,
  Amsterdam (live).   Philips 412 069, *438 283* [1993]

16 Danish Radio Symphony Orchestra, Rafael Kubelík. 17 June 1983,
  Copenhagen (live).   EMI 27 0352, CDM5 65182 [1994]

17 Gothenburg Symphony Orchestra, Myung-Whun Chung. 1987,
  Gothenburg.   BIS *CD 370*

18 Swedish Radio Symphony Orchestra, Esa-Pekka Salonen. 1987,
  Stockholm.   CBS 44547

19 Royal Danish Orchestra, Paavo Berglund. 15–18 August 1988,
  Copenhagen.   RCA *74321 20293-2* [1995]

20 San Francisco Symphony Orchestra, Herbert Blomstedt. 1987,
  San Francisco.   Decca *421 524-2DH*

21 BBC Symphony Orchestra, Andrew Davis. February 1990,
  London.   Virgin Classics *VC7 59618-2*

22 Gothenburg Symphony Orchestra, Neeme Järvi, May 1991,
  Gothenburg.   Deutsche Grammophon *439 777-2GH*

23 Scottish National Orchestra, Bryden Thomson. 1992.
                Chandos *CHAN 9067*

24   National Symphony Orchestra of Ireland, Adrian Leaper. 18–19
     November 1992, Dublin.   Naxos *8 550743*

25   Odense Symphony Orchestra, Edward Serov, June 1993.
                                                   Kontrapunkt *32171*

26   Royal Stockholm Philharmonic Orchestra, Gennadi Rozhdestven-
     sky. 1993.   Chandos *CHAN 9367*

Nielsen conducted his Fifth Symphony on at least five occasions (see
above, pp. 80–1), and in the last five years of his life he took a lively interest in the new medium of radio broadcasting. None of his performances
was ever recorded, however, either commercially or for radio. However,
four of the conductors and two of the orchestras listed above can claim
some direct link to Nielsen, namely Georg Høeberg, Erik Tuxen,
Thomas Jensen, Jascha Horenstein, the Danish Radio Symphony
Orchestra and the Gothenburg Symphony Orchestra.

1 Høeberg's association with Nielsen was particularly close. For four
years he played the violin in the Royal Orchestra, sitting in the second
violins at the desk behind Nielsen himself and sharing opinions as to the
quality of the music being performed. His career as conductor brought
him into rivalry with Nielsen, and the Royal Theatre's apparent favour-
ing of Høeberg was one main factor in Nielsen's resignation.[35] Nevertheless relations between the two men were always good. Høeberg
conducted a performance of 'The Inextinguishable' in Berlin a fortnight
after Nielsen conducted his Fifth there, and he directed the première of
Springtime on Fyn, with 900 singers. The only recorded comment of
Nielsen's on Høeberg's interpretations of his music was that 'he takes
the slow parts too slowly and the fast ones too fast, no matter how much I
preach to him'.[36]
     The recording should be of interest in that it is the only one to make no
reference to the revised score (Tuxen in 1950 was already incorporating
several of his own revisions, although probably using the original parts).
However, Høeberg makes far more drastic alterations to the text than
does Tuxen in the published revision. For instance, in the *allegro giusto*
he has the cymbal played with soft sticks rather than *col legno*, creating a

huge aural cloud; at the climax of the *adagio* he doubles the violin line at the upper octave; and on the very last note of the work he has the timpani perform a roll. Other remarkable features are huge agogic accents (e.g. at fig. 97) and sudden shifts of tempo (e.g. slowings at figs. 49 and 102 to around dotted minim=48). His slowing for the *tranquillo* markings in the first movement at fig. 16 is echoed by Tuxen (though not by Jensen). A remarkable coincidence is that the second clarinet misses his entry four bars before that point in both this and Tuxen's Paris performance. It is curious that the flutes seem not to have used their B foot joints at fig. ^{2}39 and yet have acquired them for fig. ^{3}92. One of Hoeberg's initiatives which works well, and which is echoed by several conductors in recent years, is to let the coda of the second movement move forward (from fig. 110, pushed to dotted minim=90), and a *più mosso* marking is found in some of the surviving BM parts.[37] On the whole though, Høeberg's interpretation remains a curiosity.

2, 3, 5 Erik Tuxen's 1950 Edinburgh Festival performance was instrumental in putting Nielsen on the international musical map after the Second World War. It is a significantly superior performance to the studio recording he made earlier in the year – in particular the *tempo giusto* is more intense from the entry of the side drum, and the *allegro* is far less circumspect. However, the 1955 Paris performance is a further improvement, especially in finding greater poetry in the *andante*. In all three recordings Tuxen is especially illuminating in the 'vegetative' mood of the opening – slightly under the marked tempo, indifferent without being stagnant, suggesting a kind of out-of-body experience. It seems likely that the 1950 performances used the unrevised score and parts, with a few added markings, but that the 1955 performance was from the new materials (compare the passage fig. 60–3, where the Paris performance is the only one to add timpani). Perhaps significant in this connection is the fact that the Paris performance is the only one in which the string quavers of the second movement sound entirely comfortable.

4 Thomas Jensen was a theory pupil of Nielsen's during his studies at the Copenhagen Conservatoire. From 1920–7 he played cello in the Tivoli Orchestra, assiduously attending Nielsen's rehearsals when he conducted his own symphonies, and he is reported to have had a good memory for Nielsen's tempos.[38] His recording is superbly structured and paced, nicely poised in character, and tonally well blended, to the point of almost emasculating the side drum. Especially fine are the 'limbo' section from fig. 22, the problematic link to the *adagio* and the fiery character of the *allegro* where the strings are pushed to their limits. The 'mad' fugue is properly reckless and grows to a pitch of real alarm.

6 Bernstein's 1962 recording marked a crucial breakthrough for the international appreciation of Nielsen's music.[39] It was the first time a major international conductor had recorded any of his work, and the disc was a huge success, despite mixed reviews outside Denmark. It remains, for me, the most inspiring of all recordings of the work – not irreproachable in details and not without rival in stylistic understanding, but unsurpassed in its sense of on-the-spot creation and spontaneity. It is as though the piece is being simultaneously discovered and comprehensively understood.

At the outset Bernstein's expressiveness sounds slightly overdone beside Tuxen's indifference. But from the side drum entry the clash of forces is spine-chilling. The side drum and attendant percussion loom large and present a challenge to the violins to hold centre-stage. By orthodox standards the balance here might seem exaggerated, but hearing the work in concert confirms that it is entirely realistic; a more 'classical' balance, such as Jensen's, tends to deprive the music of its special character. Such high intensity early in the structure is justified not only by the premonitory shudderings beforehand but by Bernstein's sustaining of tension and anxiety through the succeeding *tranquillo*. This sustaining of the line allows the harmonic tension to tell, as well as keeping the surface anxiety level high. The re-entry of the side drum is venomous and again brings the negative dramatic pole into clearer focus than almost any other performance, giving a sense that the future of the world is at stake.

The *adagio* is slowish but builds with unmatched fervour to a radiant B major climax, never sacrificing the blend of the full orchestral texture. Bernstein has the side drum enter in the most effective manner at slightly more than double the prevailing tempo (crotchet=136 against 60). And he has the most subtle way with the post-climax, saving energy for the re-confirming climax at fig. [1]38.

Bernstein's account of the second movement is the only one to generate a sense of danger at the same time as exhilaration. There is a touch of aggression from the outset and the violins have to hang on for dear life rather than merely demonstrate virtuosity. Their underpinning quavers from fig. [5]53 are admittedly far from *ppp*, but the effect is a tremendous long dramatic line and a sickening clash of forces prior to the collapse. Bernstein is also one of the few who manage the *un poco di più* at fig. 64 effectively (although the strings' quavers are not perfectly together). Section **B** is truly a fugue from hell, baring its teeth and almost careering off the rails. The 'sane' fugue could have more sense of hush, but every stage of the interpretation builds convincingly on the previous one, and the final coda, accelerating to dotted minim=96, combines hurtling tempo with weight of tone. The result is an irrepressible ecstasy in which virtuosity and panache, insight into character and structure, are united.

8, 10 Horenstein prepared the ISCM performance for Furtwängler in 1927 and the Unicorn–Kanchana LP sleeve-note claims that his recording reinstates the original edition. However, there is little or no sign of this. One interesting point is that Horenstein has the tambourine in the first movement hit and shaken rather than rubbed round the rim. The side drum cadenza is the finest of all, however – reaching a frenzy 'too early' but building on it with remarkable ferocity. The rest of the Unicorn–Kanchana performance sounds under-rehearsed. The first oboe entry at fig. 8^2 triggers the second to play its music from fig. 10, fourteen bars too soon; the side drum enters a bar early at fig. 34, stops, and starts again in the correct place. The later BBC recording is less conspicuously flawed, but discipline is still slack, and although the second movement is rather less limp in tempo it is still under-characterised.

11 Ole Schmidt was responsible for the first complete set of Nielsen symphonies on record, and he did reinstate a number of details from the original score. His interpretation is finely structured and conveys a vivid sense of the issues at stake. But the playing is ragged in the second movement and the recording is rough in balance, with crudely spotlit horns and timpani. The sessions took place in adverse conditions – an unheated church during power cuts. The result is a remarkable achievement as an interpretation, but one which needs major allowances to be made for its technical shortcomings.

7, 9, 12–26 Herbig turns in an extremely well-shaped first movement, but his second movement fails to take wing. This is the pattern for many of the recorded performances from 1970 on, none of which adds significantly to the above or has any points of outstanding interest. Several are extremely well played – above all Blomstedt/San Francisco (**19**), who surpasses his earlier Danish Radio recording, especially in the power of his second movement, but who lacks Bernstein's special intensity. Surprisingly, perhaps, the Odense Symphony Orchestra with Edward Serov (the first conductor to perform the work in Russia) are also very fine indeed (**25**), with an excellent balance despite a modest complement of strings, and a convincing range of character. The Scottish National with Gibson are also idiomatic; their recording is marred, however, by two small but prominent literalisms – the misprinted flute B♭ at ^{1}3 and the omission of the clarinet's tie at fig. $^{2-1}$22. Bryden Thomson is solid but lacking in poetry in the *adagio* and the *andante* (**22**).

Hearing the less successful recordings of the work reveals a number of common traps. The *tempo giusto* of the first movement tends to sound either superficial (Kletzki, Kondrashin, Järvi), calculatedly well-groomed (Salonen), lethargic (Kubelík), or simply under-played (Davis). The *adagio* can easily become overblown, especially if the conductor chooses not to let the tempo flow forward naturally (Salonen). The *allegro* of the second movement tends to come out either scrambled (Kletzki) or circumspect (Herbig, Kubelík, Berglund, Rozhdestvensky), and only the bravest conductors attempt the *Un poco di più* at fig. 64 – Chung negotiates it well but at the expense of low dramatic temperature beforehand; Kondrashin goes for a real shift of gear but with disastrous results for string ensemble. The *presto* fugue remains a challenge for orchestras; Adrian Leaper and the National Orchestra of Ireland are extremely cautious and their performance has the feeling of a careful rehearsal. Chung begins at full tempo but reins in for the third entry. Thomson and Blomstedt (DRSO) sound too easily in control. Headlong recklessness combined with clarity is the dream ticket, but almost impossible to achieve; the most successful performances, such as Bernstein's, are prepared to sacrifice a degree of clarity. Many conductors inflate the final *allargando* (Schmidt, Kondrashin, Kubelík, Berglund/Bournemouth).

Several conductors adopt proportional tempi in this work. There is a natural tendency for the tempo to move forward slightly after the opening pages to something above the initial marking of crotchet=100, and the only other metronome mark in the first movement (suppressed in the revised score) is the suggested crotchet=116 for the side drum cadenza, which corresponds closely to what many performances have in fact reached for the corresponding rhythms at the side drum's first entry at fig. 10. Some conductors have this side drum re-entry at double the tempo of the *adagio*, and the demisemiquavers of the *adagio* at the same tempo as their semiquaver counterparts in the *tempo giusto*.[40] Thus the *adagio* itself sometimes comes out at precisely half the tempo of the *tempo giusto*. However, performances which take this line (Chung, Thomson, Tuxen in all three of his recordings, Gibson, Kletzki, Kubelík) tend to give the impression that the side drum is falling in with the orchestra rather than presenting a fundamental opposition. Berglund and Järvi's side drum are a fraction *under* double tempo, which is more effective, but nothing like as convincing as Bernstein, Schmidt, Serov or Salonen, who all inject venom and pace by having the side drum at more than double tempo, effectively setting the scene for Nielsen's instruction that it should play as if to disturb the orchestra. Andrew Davis is the only conductor since Høeberg to have the horn play the original line at fig. 29[4]; it sounds feeble.

In the symphony as a whole there are huge benefits to be derived from steadiness of tempo and unbroken accumulation over long paragraphs – Schmidt and Bernstein are the finest exponents of this art. However, several of the most successful readings agree on unmarked nuances of tempo. Not only the *tempo giusto* but also the *adagio* seems naturally to invite some extra flow in the tempo over their first few paragraphs. The climax of the *adagio* (approaching fig. 29) cries out for a slight *rallentando*, though to hear it done with the conviction of Bernstein is very rare. Most interesting of all, the later stages of the last movement from fig. 105 invite a *più mosso*, as heard in the recordings by Høeberg, Bernstein and others, effectively echoing but transfiguring the *Un poco di più* at fig. 64. If this can be done with a sense of the music driving the players, rather than the other way round, then the result is a unique, uplifting, energising form of ecstasy. And when that is in the air, Deryck Cooke's reported assessment of Nielsen's Fifth as the finest twentieth-century symphony (see p. 2 above) seems perfectly realistic.

Appendices

A: Interview with Axel Kjerulf

A.K. What have you called your new symphony?

C.N. Nothing! (Carl Nielsen strokes his hand through his bristly hair and the bright smiling eyes look directly at his questioner. He continues.) My First Symphony was also untitled. But then came 'The Four Temperaments', 'The Espansiva' and 'The Inextinguishable', actually just different names for the same thing, the only thing that music in the end can express: resting forces in contrast to active ones [de hvilende Kræfter i Modsætning til de aktive]. If I could find a designation for my new Fifth Symphony it would express something similar. I just haven't been able to come up with the word which would be characteristic and not too pretentious – so I've done without.

A.K. But the basic idea or thought?

C.N. Well, how shall I put it? I'm rolling a stone up a hill, I'm using the powers in me to bring the stone to the top. The stone lies there so still, powers are wrapped in it, until I give it a kick and the same powers are released and the stone rolls down again. But you mustn't take that as a programme! Long explanations and indications as to what music 'represents' are just evil [kun af det onde], they distract the listener and destroy the absolute dedication.

This time I have changed the form and made do with two parts instead of the usual four movements. I've thought a lot about the fact that in the old symphonic form as a rule one said most of what one had to say in the first Allegro. Then came the peaceful Andante, with the effect of a contrast, then again the Scherzo where one again reaches too high up and destroys the climax in the finale, where the ideas all too often run out. I wonder if maybe Beethoven felt that in his Ninth, when he brought in human voices to help out towards the conclusion! So this time I've divided the symphony into two large, broad sections – the first begins slowly and peacefully and the second is more active. They tell me my new symphony isn't like my earlier ones. I can't hear that. But maybe they're right. I do know that it's not so easy to grasp, nor so easy to play. We've had a lot of rehearsals. Some people have even said that now Schoenberg can pack his bags with his dissonances. Mine are worse. But I don't think so.

A.K. How do you see a modern musical phenomenon like Schoenberg?

C.N. I believe absolutely that he is an honourable musician through and through. And what I understand of him I find remarkable. So there's some reason to suppose that what I don't understand is also good. I just don't understand it. What I have against the very newest direction in music is that design itself [selve Tegningen], construction, development, the line are completely missing. For the most part we're left with a succession of trivia [en Række Smaating], fragments, a march on the spot. Of course it can be a lot of fun to stand and paddle in a pond [pjaske i en Flod] – but that's something very different from sailing on it! When you hear such ultra-modern pieces of music you don't have any feeling afterwards of having experienced anything. [Carl Nielsen makes a lot of vertical lines in the air]: All in all it goes this way, instead of like this . . . the long line. [And Carl Nielsen makes a broad gesture, as though describing a rushing river.]

A.K. How long is it since you wrote your [last?] symphony?

C.N. 'The Inextinguishable' was first performed in 1916. Then came the war. . .

A.K. Did that have any influence on your work?

C.N. In any case I'm not conscious of it. But one thing is certain: not one of us is the same as we were before the war. So maybe so!

A.K. Do you expect the symphony to be understood by the audience at the single performance it's receiving?

C.N. An artist always hopes for understanding![1]

B: Statement to Ludvig Dolleris

'I am out walking in the country – I'm not thinking of anything in particular, in fact I'm not paying much attention to what I see or come across. What was that now: a flower snapping, a little clod of earth falling? Was it an animal with bright eyes starting there from a tuft of grass? (The various motifs are really chaotic, almost accidental – only one of them, the 'evil' motif is used a lot.) Then *suddenly* I become aware of myself as a musician: my thoughts take a definite form, impressions flood forth in me – and now everything is singing pleasantly.' (Modestly, almost apologetically, he added: 'You understand: I'm only describing how I *feel* it.') 'Then the :"evil" motif intervenes – in the woodwind and strings – and the side drum becomes more and more angry and aggressive; but the nature-theme goes on, peaceful and unaffected, in the brass. Finally the evil has to give way, a last attempt and then it flees – and with a strophe thereafter in consoling major mode a solo clarinet ends this large idyll-movement, an expression of *vegetative* (idle, thoughtless) Nature.

The second movement is its counterpole: if the first movement was passivity, here it is action (or activity) which is conveyed. So it's something very primitive I wanted to express: the division of dark and light, the battle between evil and good. A title like "Dream and Deeds" [Drøm og Daad] could maybe sum up the inner picture I had in front of my eyes when composing.'[1]

C: Analytical reductions

The following analytical reductions present the harmonic processes of Nielsen's Fifth Symphony in the light of Heinrich Schenker's theories of tonal music. The essence of those theories is that the structural integrity of such music results from a 'composing-out' of the tonic triad, in the foreground, middle-ground and background, i.e. in short-term, mid-term and long-term dimensions. The strongest force in this composing-out is the contrapuntal relationship between the arpeggiation of the bass from tonic to dominant and back (shown by roman numerals) and the stepwise descent of the treble from the third, fifth or octave to the tonic (shown by arabic numerals with circumflexes). To reconstruct this composing-out process is to understand both the uniqueness of the musical structure and its relationship to the universal principles of tonal music.

Schenker believed that such highly integrated, hierarchically organised structures died out with Brahms, and the application of his theories to twentieth-century music is problematic amd controversial. Nevertheless, it is my belief that given the roots of Nielsen's symphonic instincts in Brahms, important aspects of his music can quite properly be represent in Schenkerian terms. Deviations from 'pure' Schenkerian principles and notations express the distance of Nielsen's mature style from the Bach-to-Brahms 'common-practice' period. Such instances are the slanted dotted lines on Examples 26 and 27 below, which are intended to show the flux of treble and bass structural notes between primary and secondary status in a middleground which lies outside the fundamental structure.

Ex. 30 is a hierarchical representation of the tonal scheme of the second movement's opening allegro within an overall descent from B major through A major and G major to F minor. The reverse progression, by sharpwards circle-of-fifths motion, is shown in Example 32.

Ringed letters and numbers refer to section and sub-section designations explained at the end of chapter 1 (p. 16 above).

Ex. 26 First movement, sections A1–5

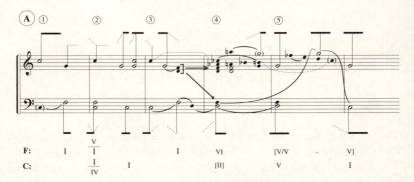

Ex. 27 First movement, sections A6–8

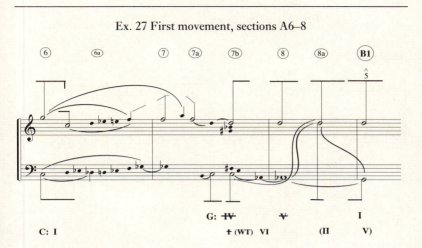

Ex. 28 First movement, sections B1–4

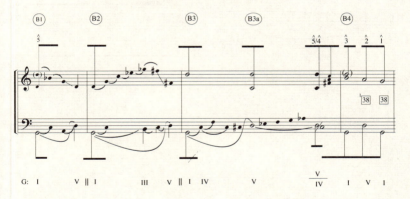

Ex. 29 First movement, middleground and background structures

Ex. 30 Second movement, section A

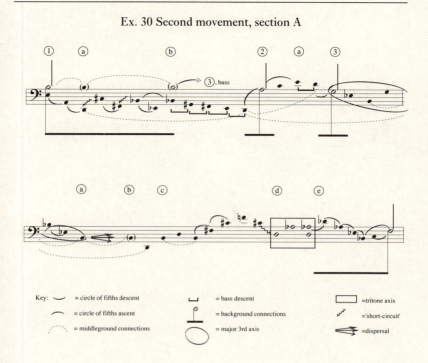

Key: ⌣ = circle of fifths descent   ⌐⌐ = bass descent   ▭ =tritone axis

⌢ = circle of fifths ascent   ⌐ = background connections   ⌁ ='short-circuit'

···· = middleground connections   ◯ = major 3rd axis   ⇒ =dispersal

Ex. 31 Second movement, section B

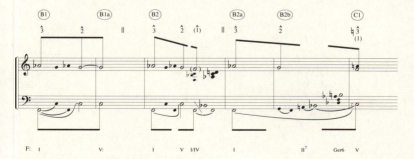

103

Ex. 32 Second movement, section C

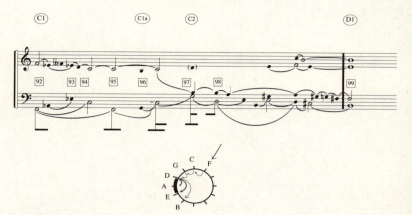

Notes

Introduction

1 B. Gilliam, 'The Representation of Anton Bruckner: Nazi Revisionism and the Politics of Appropriation', *The Musical Quarterly*, 78/3 (Fall 1994), p. 591.

2 See G. D. Goss, *Jean Sibelius and Olin Downes* (Boston, Northeastern University Press, 1995), esp. pp. 91–149.

3 See R. Taruskin, 'Public Lies and Unmentionable Truth', in *Shostakovich Studies*, ed. D. Fanning (Cambridge, Cambridge University Press, 1995), pp. 17–56.

4 This comment is not to be found in any of Cooke's published writings, however. Robert Simpson remembers the remark being made to him several times in conversation (personal communication, 27 October 1992); I believe he was the first to repeat it in print, in his sleeve-note to the LP recording conducted by Paul Kletzki, Decca SXL 6491 [1971].

5 *Carl Nielsen: Symphonist*, 1st edn (London, Dent, 1952).

6 *The New Grove Dictionary of Music and Musicians*, ed. Stanley Sadie (London, Macmillan, 1980), vol. 18, pp. 462–3.

7 See A. Ø. Jensen, 'Two Great Danish Editions in Progress: Niels Gade and Carl Nielsen', *Fontes Artis Musicae*, 42/1 (1995), pp. 85–90; M. Miller, ed., *The Nielsen Companion* (London, Faber, 1995) (henceforth *NC*); J. Lawson, *Carl Nielsen* (London, Phaidon, forthcoming).

8 An early review of his Fantasy Pieces for Oboe and Piano (FS8, composed 1889) found 'a happy gift for writing healthily and naturally' – see T. Meyer, and F. S. Petersen, *Carl Nielsen: Kunstneren og mennesket* [Carl Nielsen: The Artist and the Man] (Copenhagen, Nyt Nordisk Forlag, 1947–8), vol. 1, p. 79 [=*KM*]; Frank Choisy heard 'a healthy and genuine originality' in the First Symphony (*ibid.*, pp. 116–17); Frede Schandorf Petersen ascribed 'the frequent talk of Nielsen's *healthy* music... undoubtedly to such features as show him spiritually akin to the [contemporary Danish] poet Johannes V. Jensen' – 'Carl Nielsen' in P. Hamburger, ed., *Aschehougs musikleksikon* (Copenhagen, Aschehoug Dansk Forlag, 1958), vol. 2, p. 216.

9 J. I. Jensen, 'At the Boundary between Music and Science: From Per Nørgård to Carl Nielsen', *Fontes Artis Musicae*, 42/1 (1995), p. 59.

10 For a discussion of the particularly vigorous French turn-of-the-century debate around 'healthiness' see J. Pasler, 'Paris: Conflicting Notions of Progress', in J. Samson, ed., *Man and Music: The Late Romantic Era* (London, Macmillan, 1991), esp. pp. 396–7. Nielsen could well have encountered this debate during his visit to Paris in 1891, though his diaries and letters make no explicit mention of it. Walter Niemann's influential survey of contemporary music, *Die Musik seit Richard Wagner* (Berlin and Leipzig, Schuster und Loeffler, 1913), contained a plea for music to return to Nature, Popularity and Health, in a chapter headed 'Nation, Volk und Stamm' [Nation, Folk and Race] (p. 211), and the revision of the book in 1921 (*Die Musik der Gegenwart*) proposed that the war had actually cleared the way for this renewed healthiness and a re-emergence of Nationalistic feeling.

11 See J. F. Larsen, 'Kraften og dens retning' [The Force and its Direction], *Espansiva* [Journal of the [Danish] Carl Nielsen Society], No. 1 (November 1994), p. 4.

12 See *CNB*, p.144. For a translation of extracts from this letter see chapter 1, this volume, p. 14.

13 For an authoritative defence of this type of commentary see J. Kerman, 'Close Readings of the Heard Kind', *19th Century Music*, 17 (Spring 1994), pp. 209–19.

14 See T. Schousboe, 'Carl Nielsen-forskningen' [Carl Nielsen Research], *Musik og forskning*, 16 (1990/1), p. 25.

15 For explicit attacks see, for example, H. Lenz, 'Carl Nielsen – "et stridens æble"' [Carl Nielsen – a Bone of Contention], *Dansk musiktidsskrift*, 29 (1954), pp. 86–8. Implicit ones come from writers who point to Nielsen's move from tonality-derived to theme-derived attitudes to form, for example J. Maegaard, 'Den sene Carl Nielsen' [Nielsen's late works], *Dansk musiktidsskrift*, 28 (1953), p. 78, and N. Schiørring, *Musikkens historie i Danmark* (Copenhagen, Politikens Forlag, 1978), vol. 3, p. 138. Followers of Simpson's approach include Hugh Ottaway in his chapter on Nielsen in *The Symphony*, ed. R. Simpson (London, Penguin, 1967), vol. 2, pp. 52–79.

16 The most sophisticated Danish interpretation is to be found in J. I. Jensen, *Carl Nielsen: Danskeren* (Copenhagen, Gyldendal, 1991), pp. 360–85.

17 *KM*, vol. 1, p. 177.

18 See B. Bjørnum and K. Møllerhøj, *Carl Nielsens samling: Katalog over komponistens musikhåndskrifter i Det kongelige Bibliotek* [The Carl Nielsen Collection: Catalogue of the Composer's Music Manuscripts in the Royal Library] (Copenhagen, Museum Tusculanums Forlag, 1992), pp. 60–1.

1 Tradition and renewal

1 He completed only the first movement, now (misleadingly) known as *Symphonic Rhapsody*, FS7.

2 Quoted by M. Kennedy, 'Prometheus Unbound: The British Musical Renaissance 1880–1914', in D. Fraser, ed., *Fairest Isle* (London, BBC, 1995), p. 68.

3 'Symfonien er død – musiken leve!', *Dansk musiktidsskrift*, 15/2 (February 1940), pp. 21–3.

4 'Criteria for the Evaluation of Music' [1946], in L. Stein, ed., *Style and Idea* (London, Faber, 1975), p. 136.

5 See R. Morgan, 'The Modern Age', in his *Modern Times* (London, Macmillan, 1993), pp. 1–2, 8–17.

6 *Modern Times* (New York, Harper and Row, 1985), p. 18.

7 The last part of his unrealised symphony of 1912–14 became the incomplete oratorio *Die Jakobsleiter*. For an illuminating commentary see J. and D. Crawford, *Expressionism in Twentieth-Century Music* (Bloomington and Indianapolis, Indiana University Press, 1993), pp. 87–93.

8 See N. Slonimsky, *Music since 1900*, 5th edn (New York, Schirmer, 1994), pp. 222–3. In Slonimsky's year-by-year chronicle, covering a wide range of musical events, it is remarkable how few of the cited works bear any relation to the events of the First World War.

9 See D. Cox, 'The Symphony in France', in R. Layton, ed., *A Companion to the Symphony* (London, Simon and Schuster, 1993), p. 208. The ethical content of the French symphony was inherited most notably by a Swiss, Arthur Honegger, whose Second Symphony reflects his experiences in 1941 German-occupied Paris, and whose Third, the *Symphonie liturgique*, sets out to symbolise 'the reaction of modern man against the tide of barbarity, stupidity, suffering, mechanization and bureaucracy which had assailed him for several years' (*ibid.*, p. 211).

10 See Nielsen, *My Childhood* (London, Chester, 1953), pp. 76–7.

11 I have begun to study the C minor: so closely that I can write it out from memory... The more you study the symphony the greater it becomes. You could well believe that the score had fallen from heaven.' *DB*, p. 24.

12 See S. Martinotti, 'Sibelius e Nielsen nel sinfonismo nordico', *Chigiana*, 22 (1965), pp. 109–31 (esp. pp. 126–7).

13 V. Kappel, *Contemporary Danish Composers* (Copenhagen, Det Danske Selskab, 1967), p. 46. See also Martinotti, 'Sibelius e Nielsen', p. 130; E. Jacobsen and V. Kappel, *Musikkens mestre: Danske komponister* (Copenhagen, Jul Gjellerups Forlag, 1947), p. 350; H. Truscott, 'The Piano Music of Carl Nielsen', *The Chesterian*, 34 (Spring 1960), p. 105.

14 See V. Murtomäki, *Symphonic Unity: The Development of Formal Thinking in the Symphonies of Sibelius* (Helsinki, University of Helsinki, 1993), p. 2.

15 C. Dahlhaus, *Nineteenth-Century Music* (Berkeley, University of California Press, 1989), pp. 366–7.

16 J. Hepokoski, *Sibelius: Symphony No. 5* (Cambridge, Cambridge University Press, 1993), esp. chapter 1; cited from pp. 3–4.

17 Nielsen's own reified view of sonata form may be inferred from his remarks on Mozart and Beethoven – see the essay 'Mozart and our Time', in *LM*, p. 16.

18 Hepokoski, *Sibelius: Symphony No. 5.*, pp. 6–7.

19 *Ibid.*, p. 7.

20 Dolleris, *Carl Nielsen*, pp. 260–1, original emphases. For the full text see Appendix B.

21 For example, J. Rabe, 'Carl Nielsen', *Nordisk tidskrift för vetenskap, konst och industri*, 8 (1932), p. 426; G. Bucht, 'Carl Nielsens femte Symfoni', *Musikvärlden*, 5 (1949), p. 48.

22 *Breve fra Carl Nielsen til Emil B. Sachs* (Copenhagen, Skandinavisk Grammophon Aktieselskab, 1952), p. 18.

23 *DB*, p. 65.

24 Letter to Bror Beckman of 27 October 1914, in *CNB*, p. 144.

25 See *DB*, pp. 388–91. Many of the more personal documents relating to this portion of Nielsen's life are under interdict until 2008, at the request of his daughter Irmelin Eggert Møller.

26 F. Mathiassen, *Livet, musiken og samfundet: En bog om Carl Nielsen* [Life, Music and Society: a Book about Carl Nielsen] (Århus, PubliMus, 1986), p. 37.

27 J. I. Jensen, 'At the Boundary between Music and Science', pp. 55–61.

28 Jensen, *Carl Nielsen: Danskeren*, pp. 366–7; 374; 380.

29 Truscott, 'The Piano Music of Carl Nielsen', p. 106.

2 The first movement: dark, resting forces

1 The motto 'dark, resting forces, alert forces' [dunkle, hvilende Kræfter, vaagne Kræfter] is found on the back cover of the second movement pencil draft score. Nielsen seems to have considered it an encapsulation of the contrast both between and within the two movements of the symphony – see Appendix B (p. 99 this volume). The draft score is in the Royal Library, Copenhagen: *Carl Nielsens samling*, BOX A33.1052, mu6506.0918. It is listed as no. 66b in the catalogue compiled by Birgit Bjørnum and Klaus Møllerhøj – *Carl Nielsens samling*, p. 61.

2 'Vegetating' is a state-of-being highly characteristic of Nielsen's music, going back at least as far as the Phlegmatic Temperament of the Second Symphony. It is a deliberate sense of inertia, which may be either arcadian and relaxed – as in that movement, the second and fourth movements of the Third Symphony, and the second movement of the Fourth Symphony – or purgatorial and tense, as in the third movements of the Second and Sixth Symphonies. In any case it demands to be supplanted by positive energy.

3 See *KM*, vol. 2, p. 271.

4 '*Liquidation* consists in gradually eliminating characteristic features, until only uncharacteristic ones remain, which no longer demand a continuation.' A. Schoenberg, *Fundamentals of Musical Composition* (London, Faber, 1970), p. 58; see also *ibid.*, chapter 18.

5 Ambivalent harmony of this sort had been a Nielsen speciality from the First Symphony on – see H. Krebs, 'Tonal Structure in Nielsen's Symphonies: Some Addenda to Robert Simpson's Analyses', *NC*, pp. 214–29. For the most remarkable example, see the polytonal combination of D dorian, G mixolydian, G major with flattened second and fifth, and C major in the 'Market at Ispahan' scene from *Aladdin* (FS89, 1918–19). Nielsen was no stranger to the experience of bitonality. There was an embarrassing incident on 18 April 1914, towards the end of his conductorship at the Royal Theatre, when the anthem 'King Kristian' was to be sung; Nielsen noticed at the last minute that the orchestral parts were in an uncomfortably high key for the singers, but his whispered instruction to transpose down a fourth reached only a section of the orchestra... See *KM*, vol. 2, p. 62.

6 *CNB*, p. 133. For a different translation of this letter see *NC*, p. 624.

7 Kai-Aage Bruun actually makes the Freudian slip of giving a musical example from the 'Espansiva' instead of this passage – *Dansk musiks historie: Fra Holberg-tiden til Carl Nielsen* [The History of Danish Music: From Holberg's Time to Carl Nielsen] (Copenhagen, J. Vintens Boghandel, 1969), p. 383. For commentary on the song connection see Jensen, *Carl Nielsen: Danskeren*, p. 362.

8 *CNS*, p. 96.

9 The marking *adagio non troppo* appears only in the 1950 revision of the score by Erik Tuxen and Emil Telmányi (see chapter 4 this volume, p. 83).

10 See Hepokoski, *Sibelius: Symphony No. 5*, esp. pp. 23–6. For a musical example giving incipits of all sections and sub-sections in Nielsen's *tempo giusto*, see NC, pp. 192–5.

11 The analogy is not entirely fanciful. Nielsen once remarked on the fascination of variation patterns in the snakes in Copenhagen Zoo – see *MB*, p. 114.

12 Taken from R. At'ayan, article 'Union of Soviet Socialist Republics, I/2: Armenia, folk music', in *The New Grove Dictionary*, vol. 19, p. 344.

13 The first movement of Dvořák's Eighth Symphony seems a likely source for this and several other gestures in the first movement of Nielsen's Fifth – see, for example, the initial repetitions in the transition passage (pp. 12–13 of the Eulenburg score), the oscillating D–F thirds (p. 25), the breakthrough to G major from a dominant pedal of the tonic minor (pp. 34–7). Examples of the initial motif repetition, complete with rising minor third, are to be found in the main themes of both the Phlegmatic and Melancholic Temperaments of Nielsen's Second Symphony.

14 *CNS*, p. 96. I base my comment on the unanimous vote of three seminars of Manchester University students, in 1990, 1994 and 1995.

15 See F. Crome, 'Carl Nielsen', *Ord och bild*, 33 (1924), p. 326.

16 The dramatic opposition between diatonic and diminished intervals is also an important element in the finale of the Fourth Symphony.

17 Original emphases. *CNS*, p. 98.

18 The *cantabile* marking is an addition in the 1950 score; the original marking was *marc.[ato]*.

19 *CNS*, p. 99.

20 For a source for the woodwind dyads at fig. 23–4 see the appearance of Noureddin's ghost in Act 4 of *Aladdin* (No. 27). For a work conspicuously influenced by this point in the symphony see Robert Simpson's Fifth Symphony (opening and closing bars).

21 H. Krebs, 'Tonal Structure in Nielsen's Symphonies', in *NC*, p. 248.

22 *Twentieth Century Symphony* (London, Dobson, 1983), p. 113; *Symphonic Unity: The Development of Formal Thinking in the Symphonies of Sibelius* (Helsinki, University of Helsinki, 1993), p. 296.

23 *DB*, p. 403.

24 Jensen, *Carl Nielsen: Danskeren*, pp. 469–75.

25 The appearance of B♭ within a diatonic G major will be the starting-point for the tonal drama of Nielsen's Sixth Symphony (see Simpson's penetrating analysis in *CNS*, pp. 112–36).

26 Nielsen's own conservatoire training included the traditional thorough grounding in species counterpoint. Unlike many students he retained his respect for this method, using the textbooks of Fux and Bellermann in his own teaching (see *KM*, vol. 1, p. 225).

27 This instruction does not appear in Nielsen's draft score, but it is included in his fair copy (in Danish) and in the 1926 first published score (in French and German). It is omitted from the 1950 revised score. It is not clear where the much-repeated wording 'as if at all costs he wants to stop the progress of the

orchestra' comes from (cf. *CNS*, p. 101). For further comment on this passage see chapter 4, p. 81, this volume.

28 The instructions in the first published score were for the side drummer to follow a metronome set to crotchet=116 (the marking for the main part of the movement being crotchet=100). Nielsen had originally notated crotchet=108–12 in his draft score. See also chapter 4, pp. 85–6, this volume.

29 *CNS*, p. 101.

30 Carl Nielsen', in *Koncertfører: Fra Bach til Stravinsky og Prokofiev* [Concert Guide: From Bach to Stravinsky and Prokofiev] (Odense, Skandinavisk Bogforlag – Fyens Stiftsbogtrykkeri, 1955), p. 316. Two well-known Swedish composers reacted in a similar way to the Gothenburg performance conducted by Nielsen on 5 December 1928. Kurt Atterberg referred to the 'introductory tempo giusto' in *Stockholms Tidningen*, and Moses Pergament commented in *Svenska Dagbladet* that 'the whole first part, up to the adagio, has the effect of a gigantic symphonic general upbeat' (both reviews published on 6 December). See Royal Library, Copenhagen, *Carl Nielsens Archiv, Tryksager og avisudklip. b. vedr. C. N.s musikalsk virksomhed. 2. Scrapbog udenlansker koncerter 1906–1919* [sic]. The clippings are contained in an envelope at the back of the folder.

31 *CNB*, pp. 192–3.

32 But see Nielsen's warnings, earlier in the same letter, of the dangers of such analogies.

3 The second movement: alert forces

1 See Appendix A.

2 See H. G. Jespersen in sleeve-note to Unicorn LPs RHS 324–30 (issued 1974). P. Garvie traces a historical line for such two-movement forms back through Beethoven's Op. 111 Sonata to J. S. Bach's bi-partite Toccatas and Fugues – 'Carl Nielsen', *Canadian Music Journal*, 5/2 (Winter 1961), pp. 24–5.

3 See P. Hamburger, 'Formproblemet i vor tids musik: Med analyse af Carl Nielsens "Sinfonia espansiva" (1.sats)' [The Problem of Form in the Music of our Time: With an Analysis of Carl Nielsen's 'Sinfonia Espansiva' first movement], in *Dansk musiktidsskrift*, 6 (1931), pp. 89–100, translated in *NC*, pp. 379–95; also Jacobsen and Kappel, *Musikkens mestre*, pp. 335, 343.

4 'Om Sibelius' og Carl Nielsens femte symfonier', *Dansk musiktidsskrift*, 40 (1965), p. 113.

5 *CNS*, p. 102.

6 Ole Schmidt, personal communication, 5 February 1995.

7 Letter to L. C. Nielsen, 3 December 1902, *CNB*, p. 46.

8 For further discussion of Nielsen's triple-time movements see D. Fanning, 'Progressive Thematicism', *NC*, pp. 171–2, 185–7.

9 See his letters to Julius Clausen of 19 August 1922, *CNB*, p. 220, and to Bror Beckman of 4 May 1895, *ibid.*, p. 30. Nielsen's first idea for the *presto* fugue had the C–F fourths reversed, i.e. falling. See his pencil draft score, p. 17.

10 Period phrase-structures follow their opening idea with immediate contrast, then varied restatement, whereas sentence structures proceed by immediate repetition. See A. Schoenberg, *Fundamentals of Musical Composition*, pp. 25–31.

11 *DB*, p. 587–8.

12 For an illustrative origin of the acciaccatura warning gesture see the cry of lament in the 'Pall-bearers' March' from *Aladdin* (Act 1, No. 3).

13 The timpani were present in Nielsen's original pencil draft but omitted in the fair copy and first published score.

14 *CNS*, p. 105.

15 One of Nielsen's thumbnail sketches in his pencil draft score was for the harmonies of this sub-section (on p. 31, beneath the passage at fig. 66^9-7).

16 For a source for this passage see the 'Negroes' Dance' from *Aladdin* (No. 17, bb. 5–12).

17 Letter to his wife of 18 October 1896, *DB*, p. 140. See also Finn Mathiassen, 'Musik er liv: Om Carl Nielsens musiksyn' [Music is Life: On Carl Nielsen's Concept of Music], in A. Gravgaard *et al.*, eds., *Oplevelser og studier omkring Carl Nielsen* (Tønder, Danmarks Sanglærerforening and Th. Laursens Bogtrykkeri, 1966), p. 58.

18 Murtomäki, *Symphonic Unity*, p. 296; Ballantine, *Twentieth Century Symphony*, pp. 115–16.

19 The nearest model that comes to mind is the first movement of Sibelius's Fourth Symphony (fig. E to I in the Bärenreiter study score).

20 For an approximate classical model for this way of structuring fugal thinking see the slow movement of Beethoven's F minor String Quartet Op. 95.

21 Knud Jeppesen uses this word for Nielsen's characteristic circling-motion themes – 'around the sun'. See his essay 'Musiken', in F. Brandt, H. Shetelig and A. Nyman, *Vor tids kunst og digtning i Skandinavien* [Scandinavian Art and Poetry of our Time] (Copenhagen, Martins Forlag, 1948), p. 231.

22 This is the subtlest example in all Nielsen's symphonies of a tendency for the penultimate movement (or in this case, movement-within-a-movement) to be a kind of crucible, in which material is melted down and reformed in such a way as to give the subsequent finale 'solution' a proper psychological grounding.

23 A gesture inherited from the 'Espansiva' finale, bb. 226–78, and perhaps

ultimately from Tchaikovsky's 'Pathétique' Symphony (second movement, before letter A).

24 See Dolleris, *Carl Nielsen*, p. 360, for an inventory of Nielsen's repeated-note themes.

25 Compare with the final cadence of *Aladdin*.

26 Its presence as the first chromatic scale-degree to be heard (b. 7) might be considered coincidental. On the other hand, planting the seed of a goal tonality at the opening of a work was Nielsen's habit in every one of his symphonies apart from No. 4.

27 See *CNS*, pp. 109–10.

28 Not everyone finds the E♭ ending convincing (see for example J[ohn] G[ardiner], review of Simpson *CNS* in *Tempo*, No. 26 (Winter 1952–3), pp. 39–40. As elsewhere in the symphony the conviction communicated is obviously dependent on the quality of the performance.

29 Quoted in *KM*, vol. 2, p. 41.

4 Composition, reception, editions, recordings

1 Nielsen succeeded Franz Neruda as conductor of the *Musikforening* in May 1915, a post he held until 1927. The duties involved conducting three concerts per season (*KM*, vol. 2, pp. 105–6, 108).

2 *KM*, vol. 2, p. 169. For a picture and map location of the villa see M. Mogensen, *Carl Nielsen: Der dänische Tondichter: Biographischer Dokumentationsbericht: 1918 bis 1928 [Band 4]* (Arbon, Eurotext, 1992), pp. 823–4. An amateur silent film of Nielsen was made in 1926 at the Michaelsens' Copenhagen home in the Stockholmgade (*DB*, p. 428). For stills from this film see J. Fabricius, *Carl Nielsen 1865–1931: En billedbiografi* [Carl Nielsen: A Pictorial Biography] (Copenhagen, Berlingske Forlag, 1965), p. 61.

3 Letter to Telmányi in *Carl Nielsens samling* CII/10 'Brevveksling mellem Carl Nielsen og Emil og Anne-Marie Telmányi': Music Department, the Royal Library, Copenhagen, box. no. 30.4001.

4 *DB*, vol. 2, pp. 441, 443.

5 For pictures and map locations of Skagen and Damgaard see Mogensen, *Carl Nielsen*, pp. 789–93, 818–20.

6 *CNB*, p. 210–11.

7 For the handbill of the concert see M. Miller, *Carl Nielsen: A Guide to Research* (New York, Garland, 1987), final illustration (unpaginated). There was no printed programme note on this occasion.

8 S. Lunn, 'Carl Nielsen skildret af Henrik Knudsen' [Carl Nielsen described by Henrik Knudsen], *Nordisk musikkultur*, 6 (1957), p. 75.

9 For example the *Berlingske aftenavis*, *Nationaltidende* (Gustav Hetsch), *Ekstrabladet*. See extracts in Dolleris, *Carl Nielsen*, pp. 261–2.

10 This review may have been the source for Nielsen's reference to the Dream and Deeds motto as a suppressed sub-title (see Appendix B). On the other hand, since Kjerulf had published an interview with the composer on the day of the performance (Appendix A), the description could have come from Nielsen himself, off the record, on that occasion.

11 The extracts given in *KM*, vol. 2, p. 198 are rewordings of the original letter, which may be found in the Carl Nielsen Archive of the Royal Library, Copenhagen. My translation follows the original.

12 *DB*, vol. 2, p. 449.

13 *KM*, vol. 2, p. 199.

14 The rest of the programme consisted of milder Danish works by Peter Erasmus Lange-Müller, Hakon Børresen, Rued Langgaard, Poul Schierbeck, Louis Glass and Christian Christiansen. See *DB*, vol. 2, p. 441, n. 4.

15 *KM*, vol. 2, pp. 199–200.

16 *DB*, vol. 2, p. 510.

17 See M. Wöldike, 'Erindringer om Laub og Carl Nielsen' [Reminiscences of Laub and Carl Nielsen], *Dansk kirkesangs aarskrift*, 20 (1968–9), pp. 12–14.

18 See *Mindeskrift om Rudolph Simonsen* (Copenhagen, R. Nauer, 1949), pp. 104–5.

19 *DB*, vol. 2, p. 526.

20 *KM*, vol. 2, p. 276.

21 See Schousboe, 'Samtale med Emil Telmányi', pp. 95, 96.

22 Interview with Finn Høffding by Svend Ravnkilde, '"Jeg ser det helt klart for mig..."' [I see it quite clearly in front of me], *Dansk musiktidsskrift* 57 (1982–3), pp. 218, 219.

23 Dolleris, *Carl Nielsen*, p. 308. Another version of the story was that Furtwängler had asked for the clarinet to be 'more exalted, more temperamental'. See 'Carl Nielsen om sin tyske Sejr' [Carl Nielsen on his German Triumph], *Nationaltidende*, 31 October, 1927, p. 5.

24 *Carl Nielsen 1865–1931: En billedbiografi*, p. 47.

25 See *KM*, vol. 2, p. 195, which wrongly names Mengelberg as conductor.

26 *MB*, p. 163; Schousboe, 'Samtale med Emil Telmányi', p. 96.

27 H. D. Koppel, 'Carl Nielsen og de yngste' [Carl Nielsen and the Youngest], *Dansk musiktidsskrift*, 7/1 (1932), p. 56.

28 See Schousboe, 'Udviklingstendenser', chapter 7, p. 9. The influence on Vagn Holmboe's Fifth Symphony is noted in *KM*, vol. 2, p. 191 – this was the work which sparked off interest in Holmboe outside Denmark in the 1950s.

29 See R. Hove, 'Forsög på en musikalsk Status' [An Attempt to take Musical Stock], *Nordisk tidskrift for vetenskap, konst och industri*, 24 (1948), p. 384.

30 For example, J. Maegaard, 'Den sene Carl Nielsen' [Carl Nielsen's Late Works], *Dansk musiktidsskrift*, 28 (1953), p. 76, and "Når boet skal gøres op efter Carl Nielsen...' [When the Nielsen estate will be wound up] *Dansk musiktidsskrift*, 40 (1965), p. 101; K. Riisager, 'Carl Nielsen – betragtet fra i dag' [Carl Nielsen viewed from today], *Dansk musiktidsskrift*, 40 (1965), p. 109 (see also chapter 1, note 3); S. Pade, 'Carl Nielsen og den ny danske musik', *Musik og forskning*, 16 (1990–1), pp. 14–18, and 'Carl Nielsen and Contemporary Danish Music', *Nordic Sounds*, 2/1990, p. 6.

31 See letter to his wife of 23 August 1923, *DB*, vol. 2, p. 458. For full details of the split from the Hansens see *KM*, vol. 2, pp. 251–4 and A. Kjerulf, *Hundrede år mellem noder: Wilhelm Hansen, Musik-Forlag 1857–1957 27. Oktober* [A Hundred Years in Notes: Wilhelm Hansen Music Publishers, 27 October 1857–1957] (Copenhagen, Wilhelm Hansen, 1957), pp. 124–9.

32 Compare with 310 kroner for his monthly conservatoire salary, and 150 for an article on Christian Sinding in *Politiken*. Nielsen's state pension rose from 300 kroner a month in March 1926 to 625 kroner the following month – see *DB*, vol. 2, p. 513.

33 See Schousboe, 'Samtale med Emil Telmányi', p. 96. Schousboe has since recommended returning to the original score – 'Grammofon: Markant Carl Nielsen album' [a review of Blomstedt's EMI LPs], *Dansk musiktidsskrift*, 51/1 (September 1976), p. 34. Telmányi was not entirely consistent in his statements. In another newspaper article from 1965 he referred to Tuxen's 'simple and discreet corrections in the Fifth Symphony' as 'absolutely responsible' [forsvarlige] – 'Arven efter Carl Nielsen' [Carl Nielsen's Heritage], p. 7. The clipping, from an unidentified newspaper, is in the Carl Nielsen Archive of the Royal Library, Copenhagen: *Tryksager og avis udklip. (a) Af og om Carl Nielsen. 10. Udklip vedr. CNs 100–års-dag 1965*.

34 Responsibility for expunging the key signature for the *allegro* and for several other specific revisions has been claimed by Tuxen's assistant Leif Kayser (documentation at the *Carl Nielsen Edition*). I am grateful to Michael Fjeldsøe for this information.

35 *KM*, vol. 2 pp. 50–60.

36 Schousboe, 'Samtale med Emil Telmányi', p. 96.

37 Unregistered material in The Royal Library, Copenhagen. I am grateful to Michael Fjeldsøe for bringing this source to my attention.

38 Schousboe, 'Samtale med Emil Telmányi', p. 100. Telmányi adds, however, that in his opinion Nielsen's own tempos were themselves sometimes 'too fast', in order to emphasise the rhythmic flow.

39 See H. Lenz, 'Carl Nielsen på parnasset', *Dansk musiktidsskrift*, 38 (1963), pp. 132–5, and Schousboe, 'Carl Nielsen's Fifth Recorded' [a review of six recordings from Tuxen (1950) to Kletzki], *Musical Denmark*, 23 (1971–2), p. 7.

40 As Rudolph Simonsen indeed assumes should be the case – see his essay mainly on the first movement of the Fifth Symphony in his *'Sub specie aeternitatis': Musikkulturelle perspektiver* (Copenhagen, Wilhelm Hansen, 1942), p. 183.

Appendix A

1 *Politiken*, 24 January 1922; full text of original reprinted in *Espansiva*, No. 2 (February 1995), pp. 8–9. Axel Kjerulf (1884-1964) was a journalist and editor and son of the better-known music critic Charles Kjerulf. See also his book on Nielsen's publishers Wilhelm Hansen, *Hundrede år mellem noder*.

Appendix B

1 Dolleris, *Carl Nielsen*, pp. 260-1. Similar statements by Nielsen are reported in less detail in the newspaper *Nationaltidende*, 25 January 1922, and by Fritz Crome, 'Carl Nielsen', *Ord och bild*, 33 (1924), p. 323.

Select bibliography

Ballantine, C., *Twentieth Century Symphony* (London, Dobson, 1983)

Bekker, P., *Die Sinfonie von Beethoven bis Mahler* (Berlin, Schuster und Loeffler, 1918)

Bjørnum B., and Møllerhøj, K., *Carl Nielsens samling: Katalog over komponistens musikhåndskrifter i Det kongelige Bibliotek* [The Carl Nielsen Collection: Catalogue of the Composer's Music Manuscripts in the Royal Library] (Copenhagen, Museum Tusculanums Forlag, 1992)

Brandt, F., Shetelig, H., and Nyman, A., *Vor tids kunst og digtning i Skandinavien* [Scandinavian Art and Poetry of our Time] (Copenhagen, Martins Forlag, 1948)

Bruun, K.-A., *Dansk musiks historie: Fra Holberg-tiden til Carl Nielsen* [The History of Danish Music: From Holberg's Time to Carl Nielsen] (Copenhagen, J. Vintens Boghandel, 1969)

Bucht, G., 'Carl Nielsens femte Symfoni', *Musikvärlden*, 5 (1949), 48–50

Crome, F., 'Carl Nielsen', *Ord och bild*, 33 (1924), 315–28

Dahlhaus, C., *Nineteenth-Century Music* (Berkeley, University of California Press, 1989)

Dolleris, L., *Carl Nielsen: En musikografi* (Odense, Fyns Boghandels Forlag–Viggo Madsen, 1949)

Fabricius, J., *Carl Nielsen 1865–1931: En billedbiografi* [Carl Nielsen: A Pictorial Biography] (Copenhagen, Berlingske Forlag, 1965)

Garvie, P., 'Carl Nielsen', *Canadian Music Journal*, 5/2 (Winter 1961), 20–8

Godske-Nielsen, S., 'Nogle erindringer om Carl Nielsen' [Some reminiscences of Carl Nielsen], *Tilskueren*, 52 (1935), 414–30

Gravgaard A., *et al.*, eds., *Oplevelser og studier omkring Carl Nielsen* (Tønder, Danmarks Sanglærerforening and Th. Laursens Bogtrykkeri, 1966)

Hamburger, P., 'Formproblemet i vor tids musik: med analyse af Carl Nielsens "Sinfonia espansiva" (1.sats)' [The Problem of Form in the Music of our Time: with an Analysis of Carl Nielsen's 'Sinfonia Espansiva' first movement], in *Dansk musiktidsskrift*, 6 (1931), 89–100

Koncertfører: Fra Bach til Stravinsky og Prokofiev [Concert Guide: From Bach to Stravinsky and Prokofiev] (Odense, Skandinavisk Bogforlag – Fyens Stiftsbogtrykkeri, 1955), article 'Carl Nielsen', 315–19

Hamburger, P., ed., *Aschehougs musikleksikon* (Copenhagen, Aschehoug Dansk Forlag, 1958), vol. 2, article 'Carl Nielsen' by F. S. Petersen, 214–18

Hepokoski, J., *Sibelius: Symphony No. 5* (Cambridge, Cambridge University Press, 1993)

Hiatt, J. S., 'Form and Tonal Organization in the Late Instrumental Works of Carl Nielsen', Ph.D. diss. (Indiana University, 1986)

Hove, R., 'Forsøg på en musikalsk Status' [An Attempt to take Musical Stock], *Nordisk tidskrift för vetenskap, konst och industri*, 24 (1948), 382–91

Jacobsen E. and Kappel, V., *Musikkens mestre: Danske komponister* (Copenhagen, Jul Gjellerups Forlag, 1947)

Jeanson, G., 'Carl Nielsen och Jean Sibelius: En jämförande studie' [Carl Nielsen and Jean Sibelius: A comparative study], *Nordens kalender* (1934), 44–54

Jensen, A. Ø., 'Two Great Danish Editions in Progress: Niels Gade and Carl Nielsen', *Fontes Artis Musicae*, 42/1 (1995), 85–90

Jensen, J. I., *Carl Nielsen: Danskeren* (Copenhagen, Gyldendal, 1991)
    'At the Boundary between Music and Science: From Per Nørgård to Carl Nielsen', *Fontes Artis Musicae*, 42/1 (1995), 55–61

Kappel, V., *Contemporary Danish Composers* (Copenhagen, Det Danske Selskab, 1967)

Kjerulf, A., *Hundrede år mellem noder: Wilhelm Hansen, Musik-Forlag 1857–1957 27. Oktober* [A Hundred Years in Notes: Wilhelm Hansen Music Publishers, 27 October 1857–1957] (Copenhagen, Wilhelm Hansen, 1957)

Koppel, H. D., 'Carl Nielsen og de yngste' [Carl Nielsen and the Youngest], *Dansk musiktidsskrift*, 7/1 (1932), 55–8

Larsen, J. F., 'Kraften og dens retning' [The Force and its Direction], *Espansiva* [Journal of the Danish Carl Nielsen Society], No. 1 (November 1994), 4–12

Lawson, J., *Carl Nielsen* (London, Phaidon Press, forthcoming)

Layton, R., ed., *A Companion to the Symphony* (London, Simon and Schuster, 1993)

Lenz, H., 'Carl Nielsen – "et stridens æble"' [Carl Nielsen – a Bone of Contention], *Dansk musiktidsskrift*, 29 (1954), 86–8
    'Carl Nielsen paa parnasset', *Dansk musiktidsskrift*, 38 (1963), 132–5

Lunn, S., 'Carl Nielsen skildret af Henrik Knudsen' [Carl Nielsen described by Henrik Knudsen], *Nordisk musikkultur*, 6 (1957), 75–7

Maegaard, J., 'Den sene Carl Nielsen' [Nielsen's Late Works], *Dansk musiktidsskrift*, 28 (1953), 74–9

'Når boet skal gøres op efter Carl Nielsen...' [When the Nielsen estate will be wound up], *Dansk musiktidsskrift*, 40 (1965), 101–4

Martinotti, S., 'Sibelius e Nielsen nel sinfonismo nordico', *Chigiana*, 22 (1965), 109–31

Mathiassen, F., 'Carl Nielsens forord til "Det uudslukkelige"' [Carl Nielsen's Foreword to 'The Inextinguishable'], *Dansk musiktidsskrift*, 62/1 (1987/8), pp. 17–9.

Livet, musiken og samfundet: En bog om Carl Nielsen [Life, Music and Society: a Book about Carl Nielsen] (Århus, PubliMus, 1986)

Meyer, T., and Petersen, F. S., *Carl Nielsen: Kunstneren og mennesket* [Carl Nielsen: The Artist and the Man] 2 vols. (Copenhagen, Nyt Nordisk Forlag, 1947–48) [=*KM*]

Miller, M., *Carl Nielsen: A Guide to Research* (New York, Garland, 1987)

Miller, M., ed., *The Nielsen Companion* (London, Faber, 1995) [=*NC*]

Mogensen, R., *Carl Nielsen: Der dänische Tondichter: Biographischer Dokumentationsbericht: 1918 bis 1928* [Vol. 4] (Arbon, Verlag Eurotext, 1992)

Mokhov, N., 'O tvorchestve Karla Nil'sena' [The Works of Carl Nielsen], *Sovetskaya muzïka* (6/1981), 121–8.

Møller, I. E., and Meyer, T., eds., *Carl Nielsens breve* [Carl Nielsen's Letters] (Copenhagen, Gyldendal, 1954) [=*CNB*]

Morgan, R., ed., *Modern Times* (London, Macmillan, 1993)

Murtomäki, V., *Symphonic Unity: The Development of Formal Thinking in the Symphonies of Sibelius* (Helsinki, University of Helsinki, 1993)

Nielsen, C., *Breve fra Carl Nielsen til Emil B. Sachs* (Copenhagen, Skandinavisk Grammophon Aktieselskab, 1952)

Living Music (London, J. and W. Chester, 1953) [=*LM*]

My Childhood (London, J. and W. Chester, 1953)

Nørgård, P., 'Om Sibelius' og Carl Nielsens femte symfonier' [On Sibelius's and Nielsen's Fifth Symphonies], *Dansk musiktidsskrift*, 40 (1965), 111–13

Ottaway, H., 'Carl Nielsen', in *The Symphony*, ed. R. Simpson (London, Penguin, 1967), vol. 2, pp. 52–79

Pade, S., 'Carl Nielsen and Contemporary Danish Music', *Nordic Sounds*, (2/1990), 6

'Carl Nielsen og den ny danske musik', *Musik og forskning* 16 (1990–1), 14–18

Pasler, J., 'Paris: Conflicting Notions of Progress', in Samson J., ed., *Man and Music: The Late Romantic Era* (London, Macmillan, 1991), 389–416

Rabe, J., 'Carl Nielsen', *Nordisk tidskrift för vetenskap, konst och industri*, 8 (1932), 418–27

Ravnkilde, S., Interview with Torben Schousboe, '... du skal blot gjøre store og blanke, selvstændige Arbejder...' [you must just make great and shining, original works], *Dansk musiktidsskrift*, 58 (1983–4), 2–15

Interview with Finn Høffding, '"Jeg ser det helt klart for mig . . ."' [I see it quite clearly in front of me], *Dansk musiktidsskrift* 57 (1982–3), 212–23

Reid, S. J., 'Tonality's Changing Role: A Survey of Non-concentric Instrumental Works of the Nineteenth Century', Ph. D. diss. (University of Texas at Austin, 1980)

Riisager, K., 'Carl Nielsen – betragtet fra i dag' [Carl Nielsen viewed from today], *Dansk musiktidsskrift*, 40 (1965), 109–10

'Symfonien er død – musiken leve!' [The symphony is dead – long live music!, *Dansk musiktidsskrift*, 15/2 (February 1940), 21–3

Sadie, S., ed., *The New Grove Dictionary of Music and Musicians* (London, Macmillan, 1980)

Schiørring, N., *Musikkens historie i Danmark* (Copenhagen, Politikens Forlag, 1977–8)

Schousboe, T., ed., *Carl Nielsen: Dagbøger og brevveksling med Anne Marie Carl-Nielsen* (Copenhagen, Gyldendal, 1983) [=*DB*]

'Carl Nielsen's Fifth Recorded', *Musical Denmark*, 23 (1971–2), 7–8

'Grammofon: Markant Carl Nielsen album', *Dansk musiktidsskrift*, 51/1 (September 1976), 32–5

'Samtale med Emil Telmányi' [A conversation with Emil Telmányi], *Dansk musiktidsskrift*, 40/4 (May 1965), 95–100

'Tre program-noter af Carl Nielsen om "Sinfonia Espansiva"', *Musik og forskning*, 6 (1980), 5–14

'Udviklingstendenser inden for Carl Nielsens symfoniske orkesterværker indtil ca. 1910' [Lines of development in Carl Nielsen's Symphonic Orchestral Works to ca. 1910] (Dissertation, Copenhagen University, 1968)

Seligmann, H., *Carl Nielsen* (Copenhagen, Wilhelm Hansens Forlag, 1931)

Simonsen, R., 'Folkevisen og vor tid' [The Folksong and our Time], *Dansk musiktidsskrift*, 3 (1928), 188–98

'*Sub specie aeternitatis*': *Musikkulturelle perspektiver* (Copenhagen, Wilhem Hansen, 1942)

Simpson, R., *Carl Nielsen: Symphonist*, 2nd edn (London, Kahn and Averill, 1979) [=*CNS*]

Sibelius and Nielsen (London, BBC, 1965)

Sleeve-note to LP recording by Kletzki, Decca SXL 6491 [1971]

Slonimsky, N., *Music since 1900*, 5th edn (New York, Schirmer, 1994)

Telmányi, A. M., *Mit barndomshjem* [My Childhood Home] (Copenhagen, Thaning & Appel, 1965) (=*MB*)

Truscott, H., 'The Piano Music of Carl Nielsen', *The Chesterian*, 34 (Spring 1960), 103–10

White, T. G., '"The Music's Proper Domain": Form, Motive and Tonality in Carl Nielsen's Symphony No. 4, Op. 29 ("The Inextinguishable")', DMA diss. (Cornell University, 1991)

Wöldike, M., 'Erindringer om Laub og Carl Nielsen' [Reminiscences of Laub and Carl Nielsen], *Dansk kirkesangs aarskrift*, 20 (1968–9), 11–27

Index

Adorno, Theodor Wiesengrund, 10
Armenian folk music, 22–3
At'ayan, Robert, 110
Atterberg, Kurt, 111

Bach, Johann Sebastian, 79, 100
  Brandenburg Concerto No. 1, 80
  Cantata *Christ Lag in Totesbanden*,
    80
  Toccatas and Fugues, 111
Ballantine, Christopher, 35, 66, 112
Bartók, Béla, 82
  Piano Concerto No. 1, 82
BBC Symphony Orchestra, 89
Beckman, Bror, 108, 112
Beethoven, Ludwig van, 7, 108
  Piano Sonata in C minor, Op. 111,
    111
  String Quartet in F minor, Op.
    95, 112
  Symphony no. 3 (*Eroica*), 45, 48,
    77
  Symphony No. 5, 1, 10, 107
  Symphony No. 9, 7, 18, 97
Bellermann, Heinrich, 110
Bendix, Victor, 80
Bentzon, Jørgen, 83
Berglund, Paavo, 89, 94, 95
Bergson, Henri, 3
Berlin Symphony Orchestra, 88
Berlioz, Hector

Symphonie fantastique, 60
Bernstein, Leonard, 2, 88, 92–3,
    94–5
Bie, Oscar, 81
Bjørnum, Birgit, 106, 108
Blomstedt, Herbert, 89, 94
Bohr, Niels, 15
Børresen, Hakon, 114
Bournemouth Symphony Orchestra,
    89, 95
Brahms, Johannes, 8, 10, 36, 53, 81,
    100
  Symphony No. 3, 45
  Symphony No. 4, 51
Brandt, Frithiof, 112
Bruckner, Anton, 18
  Symphony No. 5, 1
Bruun, Kai-Aage, 109
Bucht, Gunnar, 108
Busoni, Ferruccio, 11

Choisy, Frank, 105
Christiansen, Christian, 114
Chung, Myung-Whun, 89, 94, 95
Clausen, Julius, 112
Concertgebouw Orchestra, 82, 89
Cooke, Deryck, 2, 96, 105
Copenhagen Conservatoire, 91
Cox, David, 107
Crawford, John and Dorothy,
    107